Better Homes and Gardens®

ENCYCLOPEDIA
of
COOKING

Volume 11

Companions to lettuce in Italian Salad Bowl include zucchini, fresh mushrooms, radishes, and crumbled blue cheese. An invigorating Italian salad dressing adds a complementing flavor.

On the cover: Giant tubular pastas hold a rice filling featuring ricotta and Romano cheeses speckled with parsley. The ground beef-tomato sauce moistens the Stuffed Manicotti.

BETTER HOMES AND GARDENS BOOKS
NEW YORK • DES MOINES

LETTUCE—A leafy, green vegetable belonging to the genus *Lactuca*. The word lettuce stems naturally from the Latin root word meaning milk, for when cut, lettuce releases milklike plant juices.

While the first lettuce plants were adapted from a loose-leafed wild species called prickly lettuce that is native to Asia, what we know as head lettuce did not appear until the sixteenth century.

Lettuce has long been a delicacy reserved for nobility. Around 550 B.C. it was served to Persian kings. The Greeks and Romans presented it to their nobility, too. The emperor Augustus regularly ate lettuce at the end of a meal, while a later ruler, Domitian, preferred it as an appetizer. Those leaves were held in such high esteem that any Greek slave caught eating them was given 30 lashes. Fortunately, everybody can enjoy lettuce today.

Both loose-leaf and head lettuce were introduced into the Western Hemisphere by early explorers. Plants were growing in the Bahamas, Haiti, and Brazil by the sixteenth century. In America, colonists were cultivating as many as 87 lettuce varieties by the late nineteenth century.

Nutritional value: Since lettuce is 98 percent water, its caloric content is meager. One-fourth of a medium head of lettuce provides less than 20 calories. However, there are some other diet supplementary nutrients present in lettuce, such as small amounts of vitamin A, an assortment of B vitamins, and minerals.

How lettuce is produced: Unlike many other vegetables, commercially grown lettuce is started first in greenhouses. The seedlings are then transplanted into the fields.

Lettuce growth is markedly affected by weather conditions. An optimum situation calls for daily temperatures of between 55° and 60° and an adequate water supply. Low temperatures can greatly reduce lettuce development and its subsequent harvest.

The harvesting is controlled to enable quality lettuce to be transported throughout the United States. Much of this harvesting is done by hand, although mechanical harvesters are making inroads into the procedure resulting in lower labor costs.

In hand-picking, experienced personnel select and cut the large, moderately firm heads or well-developed headless plants and place them on conveyor belts in the fields. Upon reaching a centralized location in the field, the lettuce is packed for shipment. This field-packing step ensures the maintenance of the lettuce quality. The packed lettuce is subsequently transported to special plants where the produce is vacuum-cooled. This amazing process reduces the temperature of the lettuce to 32° to 34° within a half hour.

Types of lettuce: Lettuce is usually grouped according to how the leaves form on the plant. The main types include crisphead, butterhead, romaine, and leaf lettuce.

Crisphead, better known as iceberg lettuce, is the most popular and widely known variety. Eighty-five percent of the United States' iceberg lettuce crop is produced in California and Arizona. The leaves grow in fairly tight, large, round heads. The outer leaves are a medium green; the inner ones, a pale green. Iceberg lettuce is preferred by many people because of its sweet, mild flavor and good keeping quality.

The butterhead varieties, which include Boston and Bibb lettuce, are grown commercially mainly in the East and South. Like iceberg lettuce, these are head-forming varieties, but they develop smaller heads with a softer texture. The leaves are rich green and cup-shaped. The inner portions are noted for their buttery or oil-like feel. Butterhead lettuce is noted for its sweet and delicate flavor.

Romaine, also called cos lettuce, is also grown primarily in the East and South. The most obvious identifying characteristic of this head-forming variety is its long, cylindrical shape. The crisp dark green leaves overlap and fold loosely around the core. Romaine has a sharper, stronger flavor than many other varieties.

Leaf lettuce, including green and red leaf lettuce and salad bowl lettuce, is so named because the leaves branch off loosely from the stem and form no head. Leaf varieties are popular home-grown foods. The leaves are broad, tender, and smooth with their color depending on the variety. Their flavor is sweet and delicate.

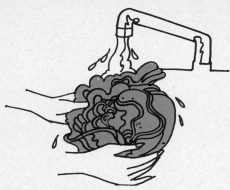

Before storing lettuce, remove discolored or wilted leaves and core. Rinse briefly under cold running water, then drain well.

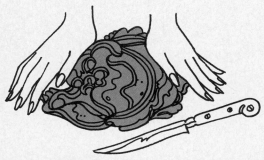

To prepare lettuce cups, first place the lettuce head, with base down, on a cutting surface. With palms of hands, gently press and push the head from side to side to loosen the leaves. Remove the lettuce cups gently.

After leaf lettuce has been washed, toss and drain the greens in paper toweling or in a kitchen towel. Use dry toweling or a rack to drain the leaves more thoroughly. Dressing will coat well-drained lettuce evenly, whereas excess water dilutes dressing.

How to select: In addition to depending on preferred flavor, selecting lettuce also reflects seasonal availability as well as quality of the food.

With the advent of modern production and marketing techniques, a wider selection of lettuce varieties is available to the homemaker. Throughout the country, iceberg lettuce is supplied to supermarkets all year. Availability of other varieties is much more seasonal. Leaf lettuce, being the most perishable variety, is often available from local sources only.

Quality is determined largely by the appearance of the leaves and, with head-forming varieties, the condition of the heads. Iceberg and romaine leaves should be quite crisp; leaves of other varieties should be slightly softer but not wilted. Good color for the variety and a lack of decay are additional quality signs. Slight discoloration of outer leaf edges does not greatly affect quality, but large "rusted" areas should be avoided. The best head varieties are medium in weight for their size. Iceberg heads will give to slight pressure; butterheads will be a bit softer.

How to prepare and store: All lettuce is highly perishable, although storage time varies with the individual variety. Iceberg and romaine can be stored successfully about one week; butterhead and leaf lettuce will keep only a few days. For maximum storage life, preparation prior to storage as well as the correct storage method itself are vitally important.

To retain the crispness and freshness of lettuce leaves, perform these few operations right after marketing. Wash the lettuce under cold running water and drain it well. Then, remove the core and less tender areas of the leaves.

If head lettuce is to be used for lettuce cups, now is the time to separate the cups. Either of two methods may be used: 1. To loosen the leaves run cold water through the hole where the core once was. Drain the head, then gently remove the cups from the head. 2. Place the drained head of lettuce on a working surface. With palms of hands press gently, pushing from side to side, to loosen the leaves. Then, carefully remove the cups from the head.

For easy core removal, smack stem end of rinsed and drained lettuce head on counter top. Twist the core, and it comes right out.

For storage, enclose lettuce in cellophane wrap or plastic and refrigerate in the crisper. If possible, place lettuce away from fresh fruit to prevent its leaves from absorbing unwanted flavors.

When you are ready to use the lettuce, simply discard any discolored or wilted portions of the leaves. Use as lettuce cups or prepare torn leaves, wedges, crosswise slices, chunks, or shreds.

How to use: To most Americans, lettuce is "queen of the salad bowl." As the main salad green, it can be cut into an eating portion, torn and tossed, or torn and wilted. As a background flavor, lettuce is used as a salad bowl or relish plate liner and as a deliciously crunchy sandwich addition.

Cooked lettuce is delicious, too. Cook any variety in boiling, salted water for one or two minutes and then dress with a cheese or hollandaise sauce; crumbled bacon; browned, buttered bread crumbs; toasted sesame seeds; or herb-flavored butter.

In other countries, lettuce has been esteemed as a cooked vegetable for many years. French cooks braise and cream lettuce, use it in soufflés, or stuff the heads for a hot vegetable. In Spain, shredded lettuce goes into a special stew. Indians add lettuce to a dish of curried lentils; Chinese quickly sauté this vegetable in garlic-flavored oil; and New Zealanders bake lettuce heads in a cream sauce with a nut and bread crumb topping. (See also *Vegetable*.)

Italian Salad Bowl

  ½ medium head lettuce, torn
      into bite-sized pieces
  ½ medium head romaine, torn
      into bite-sized pieces
  2 cups thinly sliced raw zucchini
  ½ cup sliced radishes
  ½ cup sliced fresh mushrooms
      (optional)
  3 green onions, sliced
    Salt and pepper
    Italian *or* wine-vinegar dressing
  ½ cup crumbled blue cheese

In a large bowl combine lettuce, romaine, zucchini, radishes, mushrooms, and sliced green onions. Season with salt and pepper. Toss lightly with dressing; sprinkle blue cheese over top of salad. Makes 6 servings.

A wire basket permits quick removal of water from greens. Wash lettuce; pile into basket; then swing or shake basket gently.

Family Green Salad

    2 cups torn lettuce
    2 cups torn curly endive
    2 medium tomatoes, cut in wedges
    ½ medium green pepper, sliced
    ½ cup sliced celery
    ¼ cup sliced radishes
    2 tablespoons chopped green onion
        Low-calorie French-style salad
        dressing

Place lettuce and endive in salad bowl. Arrange next 5 ingredients over. Serve with low-calorie French-style dressing. Serves 6.

Summer Salad Bowl

Easy and attractive—

    Leaf lettuce
    4 cups torn lettuce
    2 cups sliced raw cauliflower
    1 cup bias-cut celery
    1 cup sliced radishes
    1 green pepper, thinly sliced
    ⅓ cup crumbled blue cheese
        Italian salad dressing

Line salad bowl with leaf lettuce. Arrange lettuce, cauliflower, celery, radishes, and green pepper in bowl. Sprinkle cheese over. Serve with Italian dressing. Serves 8 to 10.

Pennsylvania Dutch Lettuce

A wilted salad—

    5 slices bacon, diced
    1 beaten egg
    ⅓ cup vinegar
    ¼ cup minced onion
    2 tablespoons sugar
    2 tablespoons water
    6 cups torn leaf lettuce

In skillet cook bacon till crisp. Do *not* drain. Combine egg, vinegar, onion, sugar, water, and ½ teaspoon salt; add to bacon and drippings. Heat just to boiling, stirring constantly. Place lettuce in bowl. Pour hot dressing over and toss lightly. Makes 6 servings.

Superb Salad

Tear 1 head romaine, 1 head Bibb lettuce, and 1 small head lettuce into bite-sized pieces; combine in large bowl. Sprinkle ½ cup shredded Parmesan cheese and 2 ounces blue cheese, crumbled (½ cup), over greens. Halve 3 medium avocados; remove seeds and peel. Slice avocado halves crosswise with fluted vegetable cutter.

Arrange avocado slices; 1 large cucumber, peeled and sliced (1½ cups); 18 cherry tomatoes, halved; 6 slices bacon, halved, crisp-cooked, and drained; red and green pepper slices; and ½ cup sliced pitted ripe olives atop salad. Pour Italian salad dressing over and toss lightly. Makes 12 to 14 servings.

Deviled Beef Toss

    1 head romaine, torn in bite-sized
        pieces
    3 cups torn lettuce
            . . .
    1½ cups cooked roast beef, cut
        in strips
    12 cherry tomatoes
    ½ medium onion, sliced and
        separated into rings
    1 2-ounce can rolled anchovy
        fillets, drained
        Mustard-Horseradish Dressing

In large bowl toss romaine and lettuce together. Arrange beef, tomatoes, onion rings, and anchovies on greens. Serve with Mustard-Horseradish Dressing. Makes 6 servings.

Mustard-Horseradish Dressing: In a small bowl combine 1 tablespoon sugar, 1 teaspoon salt, 1 teaspoon dry mustard, ¼ teaspoon white pepper, and dash paprika. Add 1 tablespoon horseradish and ½ teaspoon grated onion. With an electric mixer at medium speed, slowly add ⅔ cup salad oil, a little at a time, alternately with ⅓ cup white wine vinegar. Chill the dressing thoroughly.

Lettuce plus

The unique vegetable, bacon, olive combina- →
tion produces an appealing salad with flavor that is true to its name—Superb Salad.

LIEDERKRANZ CHEESE (*lĕ'duhr kränts*) — A soft, ripened cheese made from whole cows' milk. The rich, creamy white interior, encased in an edible golden crust, is like a mild version of Limburger cheese in that it has a similar but less intense aroma and a less pungent flavor.

Despite its foreign-sounding name, Liederkranz is one of the few cheeses of American origin. It was first made during the late 1800s in New York by Emil Frey. The name was adopted from the Liederkranz singing group, the members of which were avid fans of this cheese. Today, this cheese is produced exclusively in the United States.

Best when eaten at room temperature, Liederkranz is a robust-flavored cheese suitable for use as an appetizer or dessert. It is at its optimum flavor when fully ripened. (See also *Cheese.*)

LIGHT BROWN SUGAR—The most refined brown sugar. It has a milder flavor than dark brown sugar. (See also *Brown Sugar.*)

LIGHT CREAM—A cream that usually contains 18 percent milk fat. Its other names, coffee and table cream, are indicative of its popular uses as a flavoring for coffee and as a table accompaniment. Its rich flavor makes light cream a delicious addition to breakfast cereals and fruit desserts. One tablespoon of light cream contains about 30 calories. (See also *Cream.*)

LIGHTS—A term for the lungs of certain animals used as food in soups and stews.

LIMA BEAN—A large, flat, pale green or whitish-colored bean. The plants are by nature perennials but are cultivated as annuals.

Liederkranz cheese has full-bodied and piquant flavor.

Lima beans are called by different names, depending on the size of the beans: baby limas are a small, flat version; potato limas are larger than average.

From its probable place of origin, Guatemala, the lima bean, like many other beans that could be dried, was gradually adopted as a dietary staple by Indian tribes throughout the Americas. European explorers first came across this bean in Peru and named it after the town of Lima.

Nutritional value: Lima beans are nutritionally categorized with dry beans as a source of vegetable protein. In addition to ⅝ cup fresh, cooked limas providing about 110 calories and dry, cooked limas, about 160 calories, they add excellent amounts of iron and the B vitamin, thiamine, and fair amounts of B vitamins, riboflavin and niacin, to the daily intake. Fresh limas are a fair source of vitamin C.

Dry limas: Dry limas require quite different selection and care from their fresh counterparts. They can be used interchangeably with other types of dry beans.

How to select and store: Choose dry limas that are clean and relatively even in size. At home, store them in a tightly closed container under cool, dry conditions.

How to prepare: Dry limas must be rinsed and soaked prior to cooking. Add 2½ cups cold water to every 1 cup of rinsed limas in a large saucepan. Soak overnight in a cool place (refrigerate in warm weather). For faster results, bring the water and beans to boiling and continue boiling for 2 minutes. Remove from the heat and cover. Soak 1 hour. If hard water is used for soaking, add ⅛ teaspoon baking soda to the water for each cup of beans.

To cook dry limas, cover and simmer the beans in the soaking liquid until tender. Unless foods high in salt are cooked with the beans, add 1 teaspoon salt per 1 cup of beans. Also use 1 tablespoon butter or salad oil per 1 cup of beans to reduce foaming. Do not add acidic foods such as tomatoes until the beans are almost done.

Fresh limas: Fresh limas are considerably more perishable than are dry ones; thus, they require other handling techniques.

How to select and store: Most commercially produced fresh limas, large and small, are processed by canning or freezing, but during summer or fall, fresh ones are sometimes available in supermarkets. Look for clean, well-filled pods that are a rich, dark green color. The seeds should be quite plump and tender-skinned.

Avoid washing fresh lima beans before storage. To retain their plumpness and sweet flavor, place the unshelled beans in a closed container and refrigerate. Use the beans within a few days.

How to prepare: Before cooking fresh limas, wash the pods in cold water, then shell the beans. Cook the limas in a small amount of boiling, salted water. To aid retention of the lima's attractive green color, cover the saucepan only after the water has returned to a boil. Medium-sized limas require about 20 to 30 minutes to reach the desired crisp-tender stage.

How to use: Dry or fresh limas are utilized in numerous ways as the vegetable course or in soups, casseroles, and salads. Your family will enjoy frequent flavor variations using additions such as celery seed, chili powder, curry powder, oregano, or sage to the cooking liquid or to a sauce for the limas. Mushrooms, cheese, bacon, or ham are other palatable perk-ups. (See also *Bean.*)

Cheesy Lima Casserole

    8 ounces large dry limas
    2 ounces process American cheese,
        shredded (½ cup)
    ⅓ cup chopped onion
    ½ teaspoon salt
    ¼ teaspoon dried sage, crushed
    3 slices bacon, crisp-cooked,
        drained, and crumbled

Rinse beans; place in large saucepan. Add 2½ cups water; soak by overnight or quick method. Do not drain. Simmer, covered, for 1 hour. Add cheese, onion, salt, sage, and dash pepper; mix well. Turn into 1-quart casserole. Top with bacon. Bake, uncovered, at 350° for about 35 minutes. Top with cheese triangles, if desired. Makes 3 to 4 servings.

Bean Pot Limas

    1 pound large dry limas
    ¼ pound salt pork
    1 medium onion, sliced
    ½ teaspoon dry mustard
    1 tablespoon vinegar
    ⅓ cup dark molasses
    ⅓ cup chili sauce

Rinse beans; soak in 6 cups water by overnight or quick method. Do not drain. Cover; simmer over low heat until just tender, about 30 minutes (do not boil). Drain, reserving liquid.

Cut salt pork in half; grind or finely chop one piece; score the other piece. Combine lima beans, 2 cups hot bean liquid, ground pork, onion, 2 teaspoons salt, mustard, vinegar, molasses, and chili sauce. Pour into 2-quart bean pot. Top with salt pork slice.

Cover and bake at 300° for 2½ hours, uncovering last 30 minutes. (If necessary, add more hot bean liquid during baking.) Serves 8.

Thrifty Bologna–Bean Chowder

    8 ounces large dry limas
    1 16-ounce can tomatoes, undrained
    4 ounces bologna, coarsely chopped
    3 tablespoons dry onion soup mix
    1 cup milk

Rinse beans; place in large saucepan and add 3 cups water. Soak by overnight or quick method. Do not drain. Add ½ teaspoon salt; cover and simmer for 1 hour. Add tomatoes, bologna, and soup mix. Bring to boiling; reduce heat and simmer 15 minutes, stirring occasionally. Add milk; heat through. Makes 4 servings.

Deluxe Limas

Into bowl empty one 10-ounce package frozen limas. Pour boiling water over and break beans apart. Drain well. Blend together one 10¾-ounce can condensed Cheddar cheese soup and ½ cup milk. Add limas, ¾ cup sliced celery, and ¼ cup snipped parsley. Stir in *half* of a 3½-ounce can french fried onions.

Bake at 350° for 35 minutes. Border casserole with remaining onions. Bake till onions are crisp, about 10 minutes more. Makes 6 servings.

Limas and Mushrooms

Drain one 3-ounce can broiled sliced mushrooms, reserving the liquid; add enough water to make ½ cup. Combine the liquid with one 10-ounce package frozen baby limas, ¼ cup chopped onion, ½ teaspoon salt, and dash pepper. Cover; bring to boiling. Simmer till beans are almost tender, about 15 minutes.

Uncover; cook till most of the liquid evaporates. Add mushrooms and ¼ cup light cream; heat thoroughly. Makes about 4 servings.

Copenhagen Limas

Cook one 10-ounce package frozen limas in *unsalted* water according to package directions; drain. Heat ¼ cup milk and ¼ cup crumbled blue cheese, stirring till cheese melts. Add cooked beans.

Combine ¼ cup fine dry bread crumbs and 1 tablespoon butter or margarine, melted. Stir over medium heat till crumbs and butter are golden brown. Turn beans into serving bowl; sprinkle with crumbs. Makes about 4 servings.

Chili with Limas

   1 pound ground beef
   2 10¾-ounce cans condensed
      tomato soup
   1 17-ounce can limas,
      undrained
   1 17-ounce can whole kernel corn,
      undrained
   1 cup chopped celery
   ½ cup chopped green pepper
   ½ cup chopped onion
   2 teaspoons chili powder

Brown meat in large skillet. Drain off fat. Stir in remaining ingredients, ½ teaspoon salt, and dash pepper. Simmer, covered, 1 hour, stirring occasionally. Serve in bowls. Serves 6.

Picnic perfection

← Casserole-style Bean Pot Limas bubbles over with homespun flavor from salt pork, sliced onions, molasses, and chili sauce.

Pork and Lima Skillet

Ready to serve in minutes—

   2 10-ounce packages frozen baby
      limas
   5 or 6 smoked pork loin chops
   1 teaspoon chicken-flavored
      gravy base
   1 tablespoon all-purpose flour
   ½ teaspoon dried basil leaves,
      crushed

Cook limas according to package directions in *unsalted* water; drain. In skillet brown chops over medium heat. Remove chops from skillet. Pour off all but 1 tablespoon drippings.

Add gravy base to skillet. Blend in flour and basil. Add ¾ cup water; cook and stir over medium heat till mixture is thickened and bubbly. Add limas to skillet, stirring to coat with sauce. Arrange chops over limas. Cover and cook over low heat till heated through, about 5 minutes. Makes 5 or 6 servings.

Herbed Riblets and Limas

Wine vinegar gives some zip—

   ¼ cup all-purpose flour
   2 teaspoons salt
      Dash pepper
   3 pounds veal riblets
   2 tablespoons shortening
   2 tablespoons wine vinegar
   1 teaspoon brown sugar
   ¼ teaspoon dried thyme leaves,
      crushed
   ¼ teaspoon dried marjoram leaves,
      crushed
   1 10-ounce package frozen limas

Combine flour, salt, and pepper in plastic bag. Add riblets, a few at a time, and coat with flour. Reserve excess flour. Brown riblets in shortening in large skillet. Add 1 cup water, vinegar, brown sugar, thyme, and marjoram. Cover and simmer 1½ hours.

Add limas; cover and simmer 20 to 25 minutes longer (stir occasionally to break up beans). Remove riblets and stir reserved flour mixture into beans. Cook till sauce is thickened and bubbly. Serve with riblets. Serves 4 or 5.

Limburger cheese
is available
as a spread
or in pieces.

LIMBURGER CHEESE *(lim' bûr' guhr)*—A semisoft cheese with a very pungent aroma and flavor. Most people will agree that a fondness for Limburger must be developed over a period of time rather than being immediately acquired.

This cheese was first made in Belgium and acquired its name from the province of Limburg. Today, the United States as well as Germany and Belgium produces large quantities of Limburger cheese.

Because of its pungent aroma, this cheese was once the cause of a small rebellion in Green County, Wisconsin. On this particular occasion, a load of Limburger cheeses, unthinkingly left sitting in the sun, was soon emitting such a strong odor that the local people objected, almost to the point of violence, until the offending cheeses were removed from the area.

Limburger is usually served in small quantities as a snack cheese. Flavorful foods such as dark bread, particularly pumpernickel, sliced onions, and beer are popular companions for this distinctively flavored cheese. (See also *Cheese*.)

LIME—A small, green to greenish yellow, tropical citrus fruit that quite closely resembles its relative the lemon.

There are two major varieties of limes—Mexican and Persian (Tahitian). Flavorful Mexican limes, sometimes referred to as Key limes, are still grown in the Florida Keys. They are the basis for the now-famous Key Lime Pie. However, the Persian or Tahitian limes are the type most frequently distributed throughout the United States. Persian limes are fairly large, very acid, and highly flavored. They have very few or no seeds, and are light orange-yellow when ripe. Because Persian limes very closely resemble lemons, they are considered by some authorities to be a hybrid cross of the lemon and the Mexican lime. This is especially true because of their color and flavor.

Another variety of lime, grown primarily in Egypt and not very often exported, is so lacking in citric tartness that it is often called the "sweet lime."

Although native to the East Indies, limes are now grown in almost all the tropical areas of the world. Along with many other citrus fruits, limes were taken from India to eastern Mediterranean countries and Africa around 1100. During the twelfth and thirteenth centuries, lime trees were planted throughout the countries of western Europe by returning Crusaders.

The Spanish brought limes to the West Indies on their early voyages to the New World. This fruit gained in popularity and is now of vital importance in attaining the flavor of countless Caribbean main dishes, desserts, and beverages.

Nutritional value: As with other citrus fruits, the primary nutritive contribution of limes is ascorbic acid (vitamin C). In fact, one medium lime provides over 50 percent of the recommended daily allowance of this important vitamin. Limes also contain traces of many other vitamins and some minerals.

How to select and store: When selecting fresh limes, note their color and appearance. A bright green color and a skin that is free of blemishes are indications of good quality. A lime with slight skin discoloration, however, may still have acceptable pulp and juice.

Always store fresh limes in a cool, dry place or in your refrigerator. Since the relatively high moisture content in a refrigerator vegetable crisper promotes the formation of brown spots on the lime skin, do not store limes there.

How to use: Since the lime flavor permeates any dish in which it is used, lime juice or peel is usually added in very small amounts to subtly flavor a dish without overpowering the other ingredients.

The easiest way to add lime flavor is to use lime juice. Canned lime juice, available sweetened or unsweetened, as well as fresh juice adds a delightful, tangy flavor to fruit salads, puddings, pie fillings, and gelatin desserts and salads.

One of the most popular uses for lime juice is in beverages. Many alcoholic drinks and nonalcoholic drinks, particularly carbonated beverages, contain lime juice. A big pitcher of limeade is a refreshing beverage for any hot summer afternoon and a tangy combination of lemon and lime is particularly popular in many beverages.

Garnish a plate of fish or seafood, a fruit or tossed salad, or a tall, cool drink with a bright green lime slice or wedge. Each person can then squeeze the juice onto his food, if desired. (See *Citrus Fruit, Fruit* for additional information.)

Minted Sundae Soda

 1 10-ounce jar mint-apple jelly
  (about 1 cup)
½ cup water
 Vanilla ice cream
 Lime sherbet
 Lemon–lime carbonated
  beverage, chilled

Combine jelly and water in saucepan. Cook, stirring constantly, over low heat till jelly dissolves. Cool, then chill. Into each chilled 14-ounce glass, pour about 3 tablespoons jelly syrup. Add spoonful of vanilla ice cream or lime sherbet; stir till melted. Add scoop of vanilla ice cream, then scoop of lime sherbet, and finally another scoop of ice cream. Fill with carbonated beverage, pouring carefully down side of glass. Garnish each glass with lime slices and a mint sprig, if desired.

Note: You may make this soda using 2 teaspoons crème de menthe in each glass in place of the mint-apple jelly syrup.

A double-flavored soda

This sparkling Minted Sundae Soda boasts both lime and mint flavor. Garnish with lime slices and a sprig of fresh mint.

Key Lime Pie

1 envelope unflavored gelatin
  (1 tablespoon)
½ cup sugar
¼ teaspoon salt
4 egg yolks
1 teaspoon grated lime peel
½ cup lime juice
¼ cup water
  Green food coloring
  (about 2 drops)

. . .

4 egg whites
½ cup sugar
1 cup whipping cream
1 9-inch *baked* pastry shell,
  cooled (See *Pastry*)

Combine gelatin, ½ cup sugar, and salt. Beat egg yolks, lime juice, and water till blended; stir into gelatin. Cook and stir over medium heat just till mixture comes to boiling. Remove from heat; add lime peel. Add coloring to give pale green color. Chill, stirring occasionally, till mixture mounds when spooned.

Beat egg whites till soft peaks form. Gradually add ½ cup sugar; beat till stiff peaks form. Fold gelatin mixture into beaten egg whites. Whip cream; fold into gelatin-egg white mixture. Pile filling into cooled baked pastry shell. Chill till firm. Garnish with additional whipped cream, lime peel, chopped pistachio nuts, and lime wedges, if desired.

Lime Parfait Pie

2 3-ounce packages lime-
  flavored gelatin
2 cups boiling water
1 teaspoon shredded lime peel
⅓ cup lime juice
1 quart vanilla ice cream
1 10-inch *baked* pastry shell,
  cooled (See *Pastry*)
  Whipped cream

Dissolve lime-flavored gelatin in boiling water. Stir in peel and lime juice. Add the vanilla ice cream by spoonfuls, stirring till melted. Chill till mixture mounds slightly when spooned. Pour into cooled baked pastry shell. Chill till firm. Trim with whipped cream.

Cocoa Crust-Lime Pie

1 cup sifted all-purpose flour
¼ cup instant cocoa powder
½ teaspoon salt
⅓ cup shortening
3 tablespoons milk
½ teaspoon vanilla
1¼ cups sugar
½ cup sifted all-purpose flour
¼ teaspoon salt
½ cup frozen limeade concentrate,
  thawed
1 drop green food coloring
3 slightly beaten egg yolks
3 tablespoons butter or margarine
½ cup whipping cream

To make crust, sift together 1 cup flour, cocoa, and ½ teaspoon salt; cut in shortening. Combine milk and vanilla; stir into dry ingredients till mixture is moistened and forms a ball. Roll out between waxed paper (do not add extra flour). Line 9-inch pie plate; flute edge. Prick bottom and sides. Bake at 400° for 10 minutes.

For filling, mix sugar, ½ cup flour, and ¼ teaspoon salt in saucepan. Slowly stir in 1¾ cups water. Add limeade and food coloring. Cook, stirring constantly, till thickened and bubbly; cook 2 minutes more. Stir a small amount of hot mixture into egg yolks; return to hot mixture. Cook and stir till boiling; add butter. Pour into crust; cool. Whip cream; spread on pie. Chill till ready to serve, at least 3 to 4 hours.

"One Cup" Cottage Ring

1 3-ounce package lime-flavored
  gelatin
1 cup boiling water
1 cup mayonnaise or salad dressing
1 8-ounce carton large curd
  cream-style cottage cheese
  (1 cup)
1 cup chopped celery
1 cup diced green pepper

Dissolve gelatin in boiling water. Add mayonnaise or salad dressing and beat with rotary beater till smooth. Chill till partially set. Fold in remaining ingredients. Pour into 4½-cup mold. Chill till firm. Makes 6 servings.

Fluffy white frosting, golden yellow cake, fresh lime filling, and toasted flaked coconut combine to make this elegant Coconut-Lime Cake delicious as well as eye-appealing.

Lime Torte

1 cup sifted all-purpose flour
2 tablespoons confectioners'
    sugar
6 tablespoons butter or margarine
1 slightly beaten egg yolk

. . .

1 envelope unflavored gelatin
    (1 tablespoon)
1 cup cold water
⅓ cup lime juice
1 package fluffy white frosting
    mix (for 2-layer cake)
5 drops green food coloring
¼ cup chopped walnuts
1 teaspoon shredded orange peel
½ teaspoon shredded lime peel
1 cup whipping cream

Sift together flour and confectioners' sugar. Cut in butter or margarine till mixture is crumbly. Stir in slightly beaten egg yolk. Knead in bowl till mixture holds together. Press onto bottom and sides of *ungreased* 8-inch springform pan or 8x1½-inch round pan. Bake at 375° till golden brown, about 15 to 20 minutes. Cool.

In small saucepan soften unflavored gelatin in cold water; add lime juice. Cook, stirring constantly, over medium heat till mixture boils. In small mixer bowl combine frosting mix and hot mixture. Beat at medium-high speed of electric mixer for 5 minutes. (Mixture will be thin.) Chill till partially set. Stir in food coloring, nuts, and orange and lime peel. Whip cream; fold into mixture. Pour into cooled crust. Chill till firm. If desired, top each serving with a lime twist. Makes 6 to 8 servings.

Honey-Lime Dressing

1 beaten egg
¼ cup lime juice
½ cup honey
    Dash salt
    Dash ground mace
1 cup dairy sour cream

In small saucepan combine beaten egg, lime juice, and honey; cook over low heat, stirring constantly, till mixture thickens. Blend in salt and ground mace; cool. Fold in dairy sour cream. Chill thoroughly. Makes about 1½ cups.

Fresh lime wedges mark the individual servings of this refresher Key Lime Pie. A generous layer of whipped cream tops the pie.

Lime-Pineapple Fluff

1 20-ounce can crushed pineapple
1 envelope unflavored gelatin
    (1 tablespoon)
⅓ cup sugar
    Dash salt
¼ cup lime juice
1 cup whipping cream
    Few drops green food coloring
    Whipped cream
    Sweetened red raspberries *or*
       frozen red raspberries, thawed

Drain pineapple, reserving syrup. Add enough water to syrup to make 1½ cups. Combine unflavored gelatin, sugar, and salt; add reserved syrup. Heat, stirring constantly, till gelatin dissolves. Remove from heat; add lime juice. Chill till partially set; beat with rotary or electric beater till light and fluffy.

Whip cream. Fold drained pineapple and whipped cream into partially set gelatin. Tint pale green with few drops food coloring. Pour into 4½-cup mold. Chill till firm. Unmold. Top with additional whipped cream and sweetened red raspberries *or* pass a bowl of thawed frozen raspberries for a sauce, if desired. Serves 6 to 8.

Coconut-Lime Cake

2¼ cups sifted cake flour
1½ cups sugar
  1 teaspoon baking soda
  1 teaspoon baking powder
¼ cup butter or margarine
¼ cup shortening
1½ teaspoons vanilla
  1 cup buttermilk
  4 egg whites
    Lime Filling
    Fluffy Frosting
½ cup flaked coconut, toasted

In mixer bowl sift together first 4 ingredients and 1 teaspoon salt. Add butter, shortening, vanilla, and ¾ *cup* buttermilk; beat 2 minutes at medium speed with electric mixer. Add remaining buttermilk and egg whites; beat 2 minutes more. Pour into 2 greased 9x1½-inch round pans. Bake at 350° for 25 to 30 minutes. Cool. Spread cooled Lime Filling on one layer. Top with second layer. Frost with Fluffy Frosting. Garnish with coconut and lime twist.

Lime Filling: Blend ¾ cup sugar and 2 tablespoons cornstarch. Gradually stir in ⅔ cup water. Stir in 2 slightly beaten egg yolks and ⅓ cup lime juice. Cook and stir over medium heat till thickened. Remove from heat; stir in 1 teaspoon grated lime peel, 2 tablespoons butter, and 1 drop green food coloring. Cool.

Fluffy Frosting: Combine 1 cup sugar, ⅓ cup water, ¼ teaspoon cream of tartar, and dash salt. Bring to boiling, stirring till sugar dissolves. Very slowly add the hot sugar syrup to 2 unbeaten egg whites in small bowl, beating constantly at high speed with electric mixer to stiff peaks. Beat in 1 teaspoon vanilla.

LIMEQUAT *(līm' kwot')*—A hybrid citrus fruit which results from crossing a lime and a kumquat. (See also *Citrus Fruit.*)

LIMPA *(lim' puh)*—Swedish rye bread. This dark bread, traditionally shaped in round loaves, usually contains molasses as part of the sweetening. (See *Bread, Scandinavian Cookery* for additional information.)

A sprinkling of caraway seed accents this plump loaf of Swedish Rye Bread. Steaming cups of coffee and butter balls accompany the fragrant, fresh-from-the-oven bread.

Swedish Rye Bread

Soften 1 package active dry yeast in ¼ cup warm water (110°). In large mixing bowl combine ¼ cup brown sugar, ¼ cup light molasses, 1 tablespoon salt, and 2 tablespoons shortening. Add 1½ cups hot water and stir till sugar dissolves. Cool mixture to lukewarm. Stir in 2½ cups stirred medium rye flour; beat well.

Add softened yeast and 3 tablespoons caraway seed *or* 2 tablespoons grated orange peel; mix thoroughly. Stir in enough sifted all-purpose flour to make a moderately stiff dough (about 3½ to 4 cups all-purpose flour).

Knead dough on well-floured surface till smooth and satiny, about 10 minutes. Place dough in lightly greased bowl, turning once to grease surface. Cover; let rise in warm place till double, 1½ to 2 hours. Punch down. Turn dough out on *lightly* floured surface; divide into 2 portions. Shape each portion into smooth ball. Cover; let rest 10 minutes.

Pat dough into 2 round loaves; place on greased baking sheet. (Or shape into 2 oblong loaves and place in greased 8½x4½x2½-inch loaf dishes.) Cover and let rise in warm place till double, 1½ to 2 hours. Bake at 375° about 25 to 30 minutes. Place foil loosely over tops during the last 10 minutes, if necessary. For a soft crust, brush the bread with melted butter or margarine. Cool the bread on rack. Makes 2 loaves of bread.

Tangy Lingonberry Sauce is the perfect topping for a stack of pancakes or waffles. These berries are a Scandinavian favorite.

LINGBERRY—Another name for the lingonberry or mountain cranberry, a popular accompaniment. (See also *Lingonberry*.)

LINGCOD *(ling' kod')*—A saltwater game fish living in the northern Pacific Ocean. It is related to the greenling and sometimes is called cultus. The lingcod is long and slender with a flesh having a green cast. The average lingcod weighs between 4 and 12 pounds, but some grow as large as 40 pounds. Larger fish are sold as fillets or steaks, while some of the smaller fish are sold whole. Smoked lingcod is also often eaten. (See also *Fish*.)

LINGONBERRY *(ling' uhn ber' ē)*—A small, round, red berry also called the mountain cranberry. These tart berries are especially popular in the Scandinavian countries where they are used in desserts and dessert sauces. Lingonberry sauce is frequently served on the sweet pancakes known as Swedish pancakes. (See also *Cranberry*.)

Lingonberry Sauce

In small saucepan combine ¾ cup sugar and 1 tablespoon cornstarch. Stir in 2 cups *undrained* lingonberries (about ½ cup liquid). Cook, stirring constantly, till mixture thickens and bubbles. Cook 1 minute longer. Serve warm or cool as a pancake or waffle topper.

LINK SAUSAGE—Sausage meat which has been stuffed into a natural or artificial casing and made into single or continuous links. The size of the link varies according to the kind of sausage.

Many types of sausage including frankfurters, brown-and-serve sausage, thuringer, and knackwurst are processed in links. Consequently, in recipes the type of sausage must be specified along with the term link sausage. (See also *Sausage*.)

Yam and sausage skillet

Orange-flavored gelatin is the surprise ingredient in this easy-to-fix main dish made with sausage links and canned yams.

Savory Sausage Stew

    1 12-ounce package smoked sausage
        links *or* 1 pound pork sausage links
    1 10½-ounce can condensed onion
        soup
    1 10-ounce package frozen peas
        and onions
    1 16-ounce can tomatoes
    2 medium potatoes, peeled and
        cubed (about 2 cups)
    ½ teaspoon Worcestershire sauce
    ¼ cup all-purpose flour

Cut each sausage link into 4 or 5 pieces; brown
in large saucepan. Drain off excess fat. Add
onion soup, frozen peas and onions, tomatoes,
potatoes, and Worcestershire sauce.

Simmer over low heat till potatoes are tender, about 15 to 20 minutes. Combine flour and
½ cup water; stir into stew. Cook, stirring constantly, till thick and bubbly. Serves 6.

Yam and Sausage Skillet

    1 8-ounce package brown-and-serve
        sausage links
    1 3-ounce package orange-flavored
        gelatin
    ¼ cup brown sugar
    2 tablespoons butter or margarine
    1 teaspoon instant minced onion
    2 teaspoons dry mustard
    1 teaspoon grated lemon peel
    3 tablespoons lemon juice
    1 20-ounce can yams, drained
    1 20½-ounce can pineapple chunks,
        drained
        Snipped parsley

In large skillet brown sausage links as directed
on package. Remove sausage. In same skillet
combine orange-flavored gelatin with ½ cup
water, brown sugar, butter or margarine, instant minced onion, dry mustard, grated lemon
peel, lemon juice, ¼ teaspoon salt, and dash
pepper. Heat, stirring constantly, till mixture
is boiling. Add yams and pineapple chunks.
Reduce heat and simmer gently 15 minutes,
basting often with sauce. Add sausage links;
continue to cook, basting frequently, for 5 minutes. Sprinkle with snipped parsley, if desired.
Makes 4 or 5 servings.

Star cutouts grace the top of this Linzer
Cake. Plum jam fills the rich, crunchy crust
in this variation of linzer torte.

Cheese and Sausage Rolls

An easy-to-fix appetizer—

    16 sausage links
    16 slices bread
    1 cup shredded process American
        cheese
    ¼ cup butter or margarine

Cook sausage links; drain. Cut crusts from
bread; roll flat. Mix shredded American cheese
and butter or margarine. Spread on both sides
of bread. Roll a sausage link in each slice. Bake
on greased baking sheet at 400° for 10 to 12
minutes. Slice crosswise. Serve while hot as an
appetizer. Makes 16.

Smoky Bean Skillet

Two kinds of beans perk up this barbecue-flavored dish—

1 31-ounce can pork and beans in tomato sauce
1 14-ounce can garbanzo beans, drained
1 12-ounce package smoked sausage links (8), cut in 1-inch pieces
½ cup finely chopped onion
¼ cup chopped green pepper
¼ cup bottled barbecue sauce
2 tablespoons salad oil

In skillet combine pork and beans in tomato sauce, garbanzo beans, sausage pieces, finely chopped onion, chopped green pepper, bottled barbecue sauce, and salad oil. Cover and simmer 20 minutes, stirring occasionally. Uncover the Smoky Bean Skillet and simmer for about 5 minutes, if necessary, to reduce any excess liquid. Makes 5 or 6 servings.

LINZER TORTE *(lin' zuhr tôrt')*—A dessert made of a rich pastrylike crust generally filled with jam, usually raspberry, and topped with a lattice crust. This German and Austrian dessert specialty is named for the city of Linz, Austria.

Filling this Linzer Cake is as easy as spooning jam from a jar. Crust cutouts await placement on the delicious plum filling.

Linzer Cake

A variation of Linzer torte—

1 cup sifted all-purpose flour
½ teaspoon ground cinnamon
¼ teaspoon baking powder
¼ teaspoon salt
¼ teaspoon ground cloves
4 ounces walnuts, ground (1 cup)
1 cup fine dry bread crumbs
½ cup butter or margarine
¾ cup sugar
½ teaspoon grated lemon peel
2 eggs

. . .

1 12-ounce jar plum jam (1 cup)

Sift together all-purpose flour, ground cinnamon, baking powder, salt, and ground cloves. Add ground walnuts and fine dry bread crumbs; mix well and set aside. In mixing bowl cream butter or margarine and sugar till light and fluffy. Add grated lemon peel. Beat in eggs, one at a time. Stir in flour mixture.

Set aside ½ cup dough; pat remaining dough ¼ inch thick over bottom of 9-inch springform pan, building up edges ½ inch thick and about ¼ inch high. Spoon plum jam into center cavity.

Pat out reserved dough on floured surface to ½-inch thickness. Cut into fancy designs. Place atop jam. Bake at 375° till dough is firmly set, about 40 minutes. Let stand in a tightly covered pan to mellow overnight.

LIPTAUER CHEESE *(lip' tou uhr)*—A Hungarian cheese traditionally made from goats' or sheeps' milk. Seasonings such as paprika, garlic, and peppers are frequently used to flavor this soft cheese.

Unlike most other cheeses, the manufacturing process for Liptauer cheese is often started by the herdsmen. These men prepare the cheese curd, and then this curd is transported to large factories where the manufacturing process is completed and the cheese is cured. (See also *Cheese.*)

LIQUEUR *(li kûr')*—An alcoholic beverage made of a distilled spirit, a syrup, and flavoring ingredients. The special flavoring ingredients may include fruits, fruit peels, herbs, flowers, roots, fruit kernels, seeds, tree bark, nuts, coffee, tea, various spices, and cocoa. Liqueurs are also notable for their spectacular colors, ranging from deep blue to vivid red.

Although the place or date when a liqueur was first made has never been pinpointed, medieval alchemists are given the credit for introducing such beverages. These early chemists used their products primarily as medicines. In fact, some liqueurs are still regarded as an aid to digestion. Nowadays, however, liqueurs are popular for their distinctive flavor rather than for their medicinal properties.

Monasteries, particularly those in France, were important in the growth of the liqueur industry. Monks introduced a variety of liqueurs and often spent years perfecting a specific recipe. Today, a few liqueurs, such as Chartreuse, are still produced by religious orders.

Types of liqueurs: Liqueurs are classified by their flavoring agent—1. fruits or 2. herbs or other plants. Fruit liqueurs usually have an easily recognized, predominating flavor. Apricot, peach, blackberry, cherry, and banana liqueur, crème de fraises (strawberry), crème d'ananas (pineapple), and sloe gin (sloe berry) are all examples of this type. The color of fruit liqueurs is usually obtained from the fruit.

Like fruit liqueurs, plant liqueurs may also have one predominating flavor. The principal flavor of anisette (aniseed), crème de cacao (cocoa), crème de menthe (mint), kummel (caraway seed), ouzo (aniseed), Curacao (orange peel), and Triple Sec (orange peel) is recognizable. On the other hand, some plant liqueurs (Bénédictine, Drambuie, and Chartreuse are popular examples) are made with a secret blend of herbs. In these liqueurs, each herb is important to the distinctive flavor, but no flavor predominates.

The color of plant liqueurs is usually artificial. Although the manufacturer could add any color, the color of many liqueurs, such as green or white for crème de menthe, is dictated by tradition.

How to use: In general, liqueurs are after-dinner drinks, served in small, dainty glasses, or "on the rocks." However, there are numerous ways in which you can use liqueurs to add a distinctive flavor to foods, particularly desserts.

Try adding a spoonful or two of coffee- or cocoa-flavored liqueur or crème de menthe to chocolate pudding or pie filling and to chocolate sauce. Flavor a vanilla or fruit soufflé or a custard with one of the orange-flavored liqueurs.

Use liqueur as a simple sauce for ice cream. Pour a little crème de cacao on butter pecan or green crème de menthe on vanilla ice cream. For a special treat use apricot liqueur on coffee ice cream and top it with toasted coconut.

Fruits and liqueurs have a natural taste affinity. Berries or cut up fruits are delicious when marinated for an hour or so in a small amount of any of the fruit-flavored liqueurs, particularly maraschino, or with the more exotic, herb-flavored Anisette or Chartreuse. Crème de menthe or Curacao adds extra flavor to broiled or chilled grapefruit halves. Try Grand Marnier or Curacao on melon balls, figs, or seedless green grapes; crème de menthe with pears; and apricot liqueur with peaches.

Whipped dessert topping takes a glamorous turn when one or two teaspoons of liqueur are stirred in. Choose a liqueur flavor that complements the dessert you're topping. Of course, whipped cream spiked with liqueur is luscious, too. With imagination and a liqueur, you can create many exciting dishes from simple ingredients. (See also *Wines and Spirits.*)

Triple Treat Sundaes

   Raspberry, pineapple, and
      lime sherbet
2 tablespoons white crème de
      menthe
1 7-ounce jar marshmallow creme

Use wide stemmed sherbet glasses. For each serving, place a large scoop of raspberry sherbet in glass. Using a melon baller, add scoops of pineapple sherbet and lime sherbet. Top with another large scoop raspberry sherbet. Freeze sundaes till serving time. Stir white crème de menthe into marshmallow creme. Drizzle marshmallow sauce over sundaes.

Honey-Fruit Compote

> 1 20½-ounce can pineapple slices
>   *or* chunks
> 2 oranges, peeled and sectioned
> 1 teaspoon shredded orange peel
>   Juice of 1 orange
> ¼ cup honey
> 2 tablespoons butter or margarine
> 1 16-ounce can pitted dark sweet
>   cherries, drained
>   Ground cinnamon
>   Dairy sour cream
> 2 tablespoons orange-flavored
>   liqueur

Drain pineapple, reserving ½ cup syrup. Arrange pineapple in shallow baking dish. Add orange sections; sprinkle with peel. Combine reserved syrup, the orange juice, and honey; pour over fruit. Dot with butter or margarine. Bake at 350° for 20 minutes, basting frequently. Add dark sweet cherries; bake 10 minutes.

Meanwhile, combine cinnamon and sour cream. Sprinkle fruit with liqueur. Serve compote warm with sour cream mixture. Serves 6.

Mandarin Pears

> 1 29-ounce can pear halves
> 1 11-ounce can mandarin orange
>   sections
> 1 tablespoon cornstarch
>   Dash ground cloves
>   Dash ground nutmeg
> ½ cup orange marmalade
> 1 tablespoon lemon juice
> 1 tablespoon butter or margarine
> ¼ cup orange-flavored liqueur

Drain pear halves and mandarin oranges, reserving 1 cup combined syrups. In blazer pan of chafing dish, blend cornstarch, ground cloves, and ground nutmeg. Gradually stir in reserved syrup. Add orange marmalade, lemon juice, and butter or margarine. Cook over direct heat, stirring constantly, till thickened and bubbly.

Add pear halves, cavity side up. Place 3 or 4 mandarin orange sections in each pear cavity. Heat through, continually spooning sauce over all. In small saucepan heat orange-flavored liqueur. Ignite and carefully spoon over pears before serving. Makes 7 or 8 servings.

Tiny Strawberry Soufflés

Combine one 3¾-ounce package strawberry whipped dessert mix and ¼ cup sugar; prepare mix according to package directions. Hull 1 pint fresh strawberries. Mash *1 cup* berries; slice remaining berries and set aside. Fold mashed berries and ¼ cup orange-flavored· liqueur into whipped dessert. Stir 1 cup dairy sour cream till it is smooth and then fold it into the whipped mixture.

Prepare one 2-ounce package dessert topping mix according to package directions; fold into strawberry mixture along with the reserved sliced berries. Spoon into straight-sided sherbets or individual soufflé dishes extended with foil. Makes 12 servings.

Twice-Chocolate Torte

> 1 2-layer-size chocolate fudge
>   cake mix
> 2 2-ounce packages dessert topping
>   mix
> ½ cup chocolate-flavored syrup
> 2 tablespoons crème de cacao

Prepare and bake chocolate fudge cake mix according to package directions, using two well-greased and lightly floured 9x1½-inch round pans. Let layers cool in pans 10 minutes; remove from pans to racks. Cool thoroughly.

Split each layer in half, making 4 layers. Prepare dessert topping mix according to package directions. Fold in chocolate-flavored syrup and crème de cacao. Spread one-fourth of the filling on one cake layer; top with second cake layer and more filling. Repeat with remaining cake and filling. Chill well before serving.

Melon a l'Orange

A refreshing summer dessert—

In small bowl combine ¼ cup light corn syrup; 2 tablespoons frozen orange juice concentrate, thawed; and 2 tablespoons orange-flavored liqueur. Pour over 2 cups honeydew balls and 2 cups cantaloupe balls in deep bowl. Cover and chill mixture several hours, stirring once or twice. Serve in sherbets; garnish each serving with a mint sprig. Makes 4 servings.

LIQUID SMOKE—A commercial product with a predominant hickory-smoke flavor. Used in small quantities, this flavoring agent gives foods a flavor similar to that obtained by hickory-smoke barbecuing.

Macaroni-Salmon Salad

Has a subtle smoky flavor —

- ¾ cup uncooked elbow macaroni
- 1 7¾-ounce can salmon, drained and flaked
- ¾ cup chopped celery
- 2 tablespoons chopped onion
- ¾ cup mayonnaise or salad dressing
- ¼ teaspoon liquid smoke
- ¼ teaspoon salt
- Parsley sprigs

In saucepan cook elbow macaroni following package directions; drain thoroughly. In mixing bowl combine cooked macaroni, flaked salmon, chopped celery, and chopped onion. In small bowl blend together mayonnaise or salad dressing, liquid smoke, and salt; toss lightly with salmon mixture. Chill thoroughly. Garnish with parsley sprigs. Makes 3 or 4 servings.

LIQUOR *(lik'uhr)*—1. A broth or juice such as clam liquor. 2. A distilled alcoholic beverage, such as whiskey, vodka, or rum. (See also *Wines and Spirits*.)

LITCHI NUT *(lē'chē)*—The fruit of a litchi tree. This nut, which is especially popular in China, has a hard, red shell and an edible sweet, white pulp when ripe.

Although fresh litchi nuts are available near the growing areas, only the dried or canned nuts are usually found in the United States. When dried, the litchi nutshell is brown and the flesh is black and shriveled much like a raisin. Dried and canned litchi nuts are sometimes used in Chinese dishes and the dried nuts are also eaten as a confection.

LITER, LITRE—A liquid measure used in the metric system. One liter is equivalent to about 1¹⁄₁₆ quarts.

LITTLENECK CLAM—A small-sized hard clam. They are named for Littleneck Bay in New York where once they were caught in abundance.

Littlenecks are a good size to serve raw on the half shell. (See also *Clam*.)

LIVER—An internal organ sometimes used as a food. Beef, pork, calf, lamb, and poultry livers are commonly available.

Liver, the most popular variety meat in this country, is even more highly regarded in other parts of the world. The famous French appetizer spread, *pâté de foie gras*, is made from goose livers.

Nutritional value: Like other meats, liver is a source of high-quality protein. But liver's most outstanding contributions to the diet are iron, vitamin A, and the B vitamins, riboflavin and niacin.

Because iron is lacking in the diets of many people and is not present in substantial quantities in very many foods, liver is recommended as a frequent addition to the diet. Pork liver is higher in iron but lower in vitamin A than is beef or calf liver. The riboflavin and niacin content, however, are about the same. A 3½-ounce serving of beef, calf, pork, poultry, or lamb liver will provide at least ⅓ of the daily requirement for iron, all the requirement for vitamin A and riboflavin, and almost all of the niacin requirement. Small amounts of other vitamins and minerals are also present in this nutritious food.

Types of liver: Liver is classified according to the animal from which it comes. In order of size, a beef liver is the largest (about 10 pounds), then calf (about 3 pounds), pork (about 3 pounds), lamb (about 1 pound), and poultry (a few ounces).

In addition to the size differences, the livers from these animals also differ in structural appearance and color. Beef, lamb, and veal livers have two lobes, one considerably larger than the other. Pork liver has three lobes of nearly equal size. Although the color may vary within each type, in general, beef liver is a very dark red, pork liver is a little lighter, lamb liver has a grayish overcast, and calf or veal liver is the lightest in color. The types of

Golden brown, crisp-coated, liver chunks, green pepper pieces, tiny whole onions, and tomato wedges make up these flavorful Liver Kabobs. Serve these unusual kabobs on a bed of hot rice.

liver also differ slightly in flavor, with beef and pork liver generally more flavored than is calf, lamb, and poultry liver.

How to select and store: The best single guideline to follow when selecting liver is overall appearance. Avoid meat that appears dried out or discolored. Since a whole beef, calf, or pork liver will provide meat for more than one meal, these livers are usually sliced and packaged by weight before they are marketed.

Liver may be purchased either fresh or frozen. Prepackaged fresh liver may be refrigerated in its original wrapper. Like other variety meats, fresh liver perishes quickly, so use it within two days of purchase. If liver is purchased frozen, keep it solidly frozen until ready to use.

How to prepare and use: Before cooking liver, trim or peel away any tough outer membrane. (Usually, the retailer has already removed this membrane for you.) Also, cut out any veins or hard parts that are present. Then, cut the liver into ½-inch thick serving-sized slices.

Although beef and pork livers are quite tender compared to many other cuts of meat, they are apt to be less tender than the other types of liver. This makes beef and pork liver especially suited to moist-heat cookery (braising). On the other hand, calf, lamb, and poultry livers can be successfully cooked using dry heat methods (broiling, frying, and panbroiling).

The nutritional value of liver makes it an important food that should be served often. One of the most popular ways to serve liver is in combination with sautéed onions. The subtle cooked onion flavor is the perfect complement for this meat. However, you can vary the menu and still include liver when you serve it with a barbecue or cream sauce, grind it and make a meat loaf, make a pâté, or serve poultry livers as bite-sized appetizers. Also try combining it with other ingredients such as pastas or vegetables for an unusual main dish. (See also *Variety Meat.*)

Liver

Remove membrane and veins from 1 pound calves liver, ⅜ to ½ inch thick. Cook in one of the following ways. Makes 4 servings.

Panfried: Dip slices of liver in seasoned all-purpose flour. Brown quickly on one side in ¼ cup hot shortening, about 1 minute; turn, cook 2 to 3 minutes. Don't overcook.

Broiled: Dip slices of liver in 2 tablespoons butter or margarine, melted, *or* French-style salad dressing. Broil 3 inches from heat for 3 minutes. Turn, top with bacon slices, and broil 3 minutes longer; turn bacon once.

Braised: Dip slices of liver in ¼ cup all-purpose flour seasoned with salt and pepper. Brown quickly on both sides in 3 to 4 tablespoons hot shortening. Reduce heat. Dissolve 1 beef bouillon cube in ½ cup boiling water; add to skillet with 1 medium onion, thinly sliced. Cook over low heat 15 to 20 minutes.

French fried: Cut liver in strips, ½ inch wide. Let stand in ½ cup French-style salad dressing 30 minutes; drain. Dip in 1 beaten egg; roll in 1 cup saltine cracker crumbs. Fry in deep hot fat (360°) about 2 minutes. Drain.

Sausage-Liver Rolls

Cut 1 pound beef liver into 8 ¼-inch thick slices. Lay 1 brown-and-serve sausage link atop *each* piece of liver; roll liver around sausage link. Fasten with wooden pick.

In 8-inch skillet brown liver rolls slowly in 1 tablespoon hot salad oil; drain off excess fat. Combine ⅓ cup water and one 8-ounce can tomato sauce with chopped onion; pour over liver rolls. Cover tightly and simmer till meat is tender, about 20 minutes. Remove wooden pick before serving. Makes 8 servings.

Liver Kabobs

  2 tablespoons salad oil
  2 tablespoons Dijon-style
      mustard
  1 tablespoon lemon juice
  1 tablespoon catsup
  2 teaspoons Worcestershire sauce
  ½ teaspoon onion powder
      Dash cayenne
  1 pound 1-inch thick beef liver,
      cut in 2-inch cubes
  1 8-ounce can tiny whole onions
  ⅔ cup fine dry bread crumbs
  1 green pepper, cut in large
      pieces
  2 tomatoes, cut in eighths
      Hot cooked rice

Combine salad oil, Dijon-style mustard, lemon juice, catsup, Worcestershire sauce, onion powder, and cayenne. Add liver cubes; stir to coat. Refrigerate 3 to 4 hours, turning meat occasionally. Remove liver from mixture.

Drain onions. Roll liver in fine dry bread crumbs. Thread long skewers with liver cubes, whole onions, and green pepper pieces. Place kabobs on greased rack of broiler pan. Broil 6 inches from heat till liver is tender, about 5 minutes on each of two sides. Add tomato pieces to ends of skewers the last few minutes of cooking time just to heat. Serve kabobs on hot cooked rice. Makes 4 servings.

Liver Loaf

  1 pound calves liver
  1 medium onion, quartered
  1 pound ground pork
  1 cup soft bread crumbs
  1 teaspoon Worcestershire sauce
  ½ teaspoon celery salt
  2 beaten eggs
  3 slices bacon, halved

In saucepan cover liver with hot water; simmer 5 minutes. Drain; reserve 1 cup stock.

Put liver and onion through medium blade of food chopper. Add pork, next 4 ingredients, 1 teaspoon salt, dash pepper, and reserved stock. Form into loaf in 8½x4½x2½-inch baking dish. Top with bacon. Bake at 350° for 1 hour. Drain off fat. Serves 8.

Liver sausage can be sliced or spread for sandwiches.

Bacon and Liver Bake

Combine 6 slices bacon, chopped, and 1 cup chopped onion in skillet. Cook till bacon is crisp and onion is tender. Remove, reserving drippings in skillet. Combine ¼ cup all-purpose flour, 1 teaspoon salt, and dash pepper. Coat 1 pound beef liver, cut in serving-sized pieces, with flour mixture. Reserve remaining flour mixture. Brown liver in bacon drippings. Remove liver to 10x6x1¾-inch baking dish.

Blend reserved flour mixture with drippings in skillet till smooth. Add 1½ cups milk. Cook and stir till thickened and bubbly. Pour over liver. Sprinkle bacon and onion over. Combine ¼ cup fine dry bread crumbs and 1 tablespoon butter, melted; sprinkle atop liver. Bake, uncovered, at 350° about 25 minutes. Serves 4.

Liver and Tomato Skillet

    1 pound beef liver, ½ inch thick
 ¼ cup all-purpose flour
    2 tablespoons shortening
 ½ cup chopped onion
 ¼ cup chopped green pepper
    1 16-ounce can tomatoes, cut up
    1 teaspoon sugar
 ¼ teaspoon dried basil leaves,
        crushed
    Dash garlic powder
 ½ teaspoon Worcestershire sauce
    Hot cooked rice

Cut liver in serving-sized pieces; coat with flour. Brown in hot shortening; season. Remove liver. In same skillet cook onion till tender. Stir in ½ teaspoon salt and remaining ingredients *except* rice. Add liver. Simmer, uncovered, 15 minutes. Serve over rice. Serves 4 or 5.

LIVER SAUSAGE, LIVERWURST—Another name for the sausage called braunschweiger. Pork liver is an essential ingredient in this sausage. (See also *Braunschweiger.*)

LOAF—Food shaped to a rectangular mass. Bread and ground beef are frequently shaped into a loaf before baking.

Pork-Apricot Loaf

 1½ cups soft bread crumbs
 ¾ cup milk
    1 pound ground ham
    1 pound ground fresh pork
    1 cup snipped dried apricots
    2 eggs
    2 tablespoons snipped parsley
    2 tablespoons chopped onion
 ½ cup brown sugar
    1 teaspoon all-purpose flour

Combine soft bread crumbs and milk; let stand for 5 minutes. Add next 6 ingredients; mix thoroughly. Combine brown sugar and flour; sprinkle in bottom of 9x5x3-inch loaf pan. Pat meat mixture into pan. Bake at 350° for 1 hour and 15 minutes. Makes 8 servings.

LOAF CAKE—Any cake baked in a high-sided, rectangular pan. Pound cakes are usually baked in this way. (See also *Cake.*)

Chocolate Marble Cake

In mixing bowl cream ½ cup butter and 1 cup sugar till light. Add 1 teaspoon vanilla and 3 eggs, one at a time, beating well after each. Sift together 2 cups sifted cake flour, 2½ teaspoons baking powder, and ¼ teaspoon salt; add to creamed mixture alternately with ⅔ cup milk, beating after each addition.

Melt one 1-ounce square unsweetened chocolate; cool. Combine chocolate, 2 tablespoons hot water, ¼ teaspoon baking soda, and ⅛ teaspoon red food coloring; stir into a *third* of the batter. Alternate light and dark batters by spoonfuls in greased and lightly floured 9x5x3-inch loaf pan. Zigzag spatula through batter. Bake at 350° for 55 to 60 minutes. Cool 15 minutes; remove from pan. Cool thoroughly.

LOAF CHEESE—Cheese shaped into a rectangle. This name refers to the loaflike shape of various natural and processed cheeses rather than to a specific type of cheese. Before 1940, loaf cheeses were usually processed cheeses. (See also *Cheese.*)

LOBSTER—Large shellfish belonging to the same class as crab and shrimp. Lobsters are a bluish green color until they are cooked. Then, they turn the bright red which is usually associated with lobster.

A shell, much like a coat of mail from the Middle Ages, covers the lobster's body. Maine lobsters are distinguished by two large claws. These claws differ in shape; one is slender for slicing food, the other is larger and has teethlike protrusions for crushing. All lobsters are not alike; some are left-handed, and some are right-handed.

In their early life, lobsters receive more motherly attention than do most other shellfish. The female carries eggs on the undersurface of her abdomen for 10 to 11 months. During this time, she protects her eggs so well that few are ever lost.

When hatched, tiny lobsters are quite different from the adult. Not until they go through several molts (shedding the shell in order to grow) do they look like a lobster. Unlike most shellfish, lobsters continue to grow as long as they live, some reaching as much as 30 pounds.

Lobsters live on the bottom of the sea. They swim by flexing their powerful tails or walking nimbly on the ocean floor. As they walk, lobsters hold their large claws in front of them as a protective device as well as a means of searching for food. Sometimes, lobsters dig up the ocean floor searching for food to eat. However, they are awkward and almost helpless on land without water to support their weight. Their keen sense of smell lures lobsters up into the pots or creels set out by fishermen. These cratelike traps are made of plastic or slat hoops covered with netting. Small fish are used for bait. Once the lobsters enter the narrow opening, they are not able to retrace their path and escape.

Lobsters that are too large to enter these traps are taken in deeper waters by trawlers who dredge them up. Lobsters are kept alive until time for cooking or processing.

Types of lobsters: The true lobsters are found all along the northern Atlantic coasts. The spiny or rock lobster and the crayfish, living in warmer waters, are distant relatives of the true lobster.

In Europe, lobsters inhabit the coastal waters from Norway to the Mediterranean Sea. These average ten pounds and under. American lobsters are found from Labrador to North Carolina and are generally larger than the European ones.

When the American colonies were first settled, lobsters were found in such great numbers that they were sold for a penny each and were even used for fertilizer. Through the years, however, so many were caught that lobsters are now more scarce.

Spiny or rock lobsters and crayfish are more widespread. They are found in Europe from southern Britain to the Mediterranean, the Caribbean, southern Florida, California, Australia, and South Africa. These differ from true lobsters in that they have a spiny shell, no large pincers, and more meat in the tail.

Nutritional value: Lobster meat contains protein, minerals, and B vitamins. The calories in raw lobster meat average about 90 for 3½ ounces of northern lobster, 72 for 3½ ounces of spiny lobster, and 75 for ½ cup of canned meat.

How to select: Several forms of lobster—live, fresh cooked, frozen, and canned—are available year-round.

Live lobsters are most plentiful in the summer months when they venture closer to the shore. They are more common along the coasts, but with modern airline service, lobsters are available all over the country.

When buying live lobsters, choose only the active ones. Before handling, be sure the claws are plugged. Then, grasp just behind the eyes. The tail should curl under the body when picked up.

Individual serving for luncheon

Present the guests with an elegant but easy→ menu of Lobster Thermidor Bake, tossed salad, hot coffee, and a make-ahead dessert.

Basic Boiled Lobster

Select active live lobsters. Plunge into enough boiling, salted water to cover. Bring water to boiling; reduce heat and simmer 20 minutes. Remove lobster at once. Place on back; with sharp knife, cut in half lengthwise. Remove black vein that runs to tip of tail. Discard all organs in body section near head except red coral roe (in females only) and brownish green liver. Crack claws. Serve with cups of melted butter. Or chill and use meat in salads.

Cooked whole lobsters and chunks of cooked meat are also available on the market. Fresh whole ones are bright red and have a fresh sea odor. The tail should spring back quickly after being straightened out. Ask the marketman to be sure the lobster was cooked the day of purchase.

Frozen and canned lobster meat are available in most supermarkets. The frozen form can be purchased in the shell. Buying the frozen or canned forms allows more time between purchase and eating time.

When selecting whole lobsters, look for the grade marked on the package, as this indicates the size: *chicken*—¾ to 1 pound, *quarters*—1¼ pounds, *large*—1½ to 2¼ pounds, and *jumbos*—over 2½ pounds.

Purchase about 1 to 1½ pounds of whole lobster, ½ pound of tails, or ¼ pound of lobster meat for each person.

How to store: Live lobsters cannot be stored but must be cooked immediately. Fresh cooked meat should be chilled and used as soon as possible. If the lobster cannot be eaten soon, freeze the meat. Cook as for eating, chill, remove meat from shell, and wrap. Keep frozen up to 1 month, then thaw and use the same as fresh cooked.

Commercially frozen lobster can be stored in the freezer for as long as six months. Canned lobster generally keeps very well for about a year on the shelf.

How to cook: Lobster can be boiled, broiled, baked, or fried. Be sure the lobsters are alive when plunged into the boiling water or were killed just before broiling. Lobster should not be overcooked, but cooked till the meat loses its transparent appearance.

Drop frozen lobster tails into boiling, salted water to cover. When water boils again, reduce heat and simmer till cooked.

Drain cooked lobster tails. With scissors, cut away thin underside membrane—cut down each side and remove undershell.

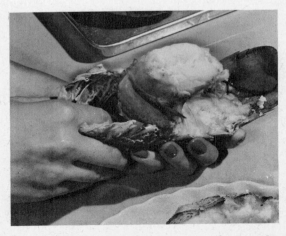

To remove lobster meat, grasp tail securely. Insert index finger between shell and meat; pull firmly. Chill lobster, if desired.

Basic Broiled Lobster

Select active live lobsters. Plunge into enough boiling, salted water to cover. Cook 2 minutes. Remove from boiling water; place lobsters backside down on cutting board. With a sharp knife, split the lobsters lengthwise from head to tail. Cut off the heads, if desired.

Using scissors, snip out undershell membrane on tail sections. Discard all organs in the body section except the brownish green liver and red coral roe (in females only). Remove the black vein that runs down to the tail. Crack the large claws.

Place on broiler pan, shell side up; broil 5 inches from heat for 7 minutes. Turn; flatten open to expose meat. Brush with 1 tablespoon butter, melted. Season with salt and pepper. Broil 7 to 8 minutes more. Serve with melted butter or clarified butter and lemon wedges. Allow 1 to 1½ pounds lobster for each serving.

Lobster Tails

Boiled: Drop frozen lobster tails into boiling, salted water to cover. Bring to boiling; simmer 3 ounce tails 3 to 4 minutes, 6 ounce tails 8 minutes, and 8 ounce tails 11 minutes. Drain. Prepare to serve (see pictures on opposite page). Pass melted butter.

Broiled: With sharp knife, cut down through center of hard top shell of frozen tail (see *Butterfly Cut* for illustration). Cut through meat, but not through undershell. Spread open, butterfly-style, so meat is on top. Place tails on broiler pan, shell side down. Dash few drops bottled hot pepper sauce into melted butter; brush over meat.

Broil tails 4 inches from the heat. Cook till meat loses its translucency and can be flaked easily when tested with a fork, about 17 minutes for a 6- to 8-ounce tail. Loosen meat by inserting fork between shell and meat. Pass melted butter or clarified butter and lemon. Allow about ½ pound for each serving.

How to eat: Cooked lobsters are eaten alone or mixed with other ingredients for entrées and appetizers. Eating lobsters directly from the shell is an adventure. This art can be mastered if the lobsters are prepared correctly. (See also *Shellfish.*)

How to eat lobster

Begin by holding the body of the whole cooked lobster with one hand. With the other hand twist off the two large claws.

Use a nutcracker or mallet to crack open the large lobster claws. Remove the lobster meat with a nutpick or small seafood fork.

Grasp the lobster body and tail with both hands. Arch the back of the lobster until it cracks. Then, separate the tail from body.

Loosen the meat from the tail with a fork and cut the meat into bite-sized pieces.

Break off the small claws and place the meat-filled end in your mouth. Gently suck out any meat that may be in these claws.

Pick up the body section and crack it in half. Use a seafood fork to eat the meat, red coral roe, and brownish green liver.

Baked Lobster Savannah

  2 2-pound lobsters
  ½ cup sliced fresh mushrooms
  ¼ cup diced green pepper
  3 tablespoons butter or margarine
  2 tablespoons all-purpose flour
  1 cup milk
  ¼ cup dry sherry
  1 teaspoon paprika
  2 tablespoons diced pimiento
    Grated cheese
    Fresh bread crumbs

Boil lobsters; cool. Cut off claws and legs. Hold lobster body with top side up; using kitchen shears, cut an oval opening in top of shell from base of head to tail. Remove all meat from body and claws; cube.

Cook mushrooms and green pepper in butter till tender. Blend in flour; add milk; cook and stir till mixture thickens and bubbles. Add sherry, paprika, and salt to taste; cook 5 minutes. Add lobster and pimiento. Pile filling in lobster shells; top with cheese and crumbs Bake at 375° for 15 minutes. Serves 2.

Boil or broil lobster tails, loosen meat by inserting a fork between shell and meat, and top with melted butter. Serve this delicacy with french-fried potatoes and twists of lemon.

Lobster Thermidor Bake

Cook 4 frozen lobster tails (about 1 pound). Cut through lobster shell lengthwise with a sharp knife. Remove the meat from shells; cut meat into large pieces. In medium skillet cook $\frac{1}{3}$ cup chopped onion and 1 clove garlic, minced, in 2 tablespoons butter or margarine till onion is tender but not brown.

To mixture in the skillet, add one 11-ounce can condensed Cheddar cheese soup and one 3-ounce can sliced mushrooms, drained. Gradually blend in $\frac{1}{3}$ cup light cream, $\frac{1}{4}$ cup dry sherry, and 2 tablespoons snipped parsley. Add lobster pieces and one 10-ounce package frozen peas, cooked and drained.

Cook the mixture, stirring occasionally, till it is heated through. Spoon the mixture into four 1-cup casseroles; sprinkle 2 teaspoons buttered soft bread crumbs around the edges of each casserole. Bake at 350° for about 25 to 30 minutes. Makes 4 individual servings.

Lobster en Coquille

Bake in coquilles or individual casseroles—

Cook one 9-ounce package frozen lobster tails according to package directions. Cool; remove meat from shells and cut in bite-sized pieces.

In a saucepan cook $\frac{1}{2}$ cup finely chopped celery in 1 tablespoon butter or margarine till tender but not brown. Stir in one 10-ounce can frozen condensed cream of shrimp soup, thawed; $\frac{1}{4}$ cup milk; one 3-ounce can sliced mushrooms, drained; $\frac{1}{2}$ cup soft bread crumbs; 1 tablespoon dry sherry; and lobster. Bring mixture to boiling, stirring constantly. Spoon into 4 individual baking shells or casseroles.

Combine $\frac{1}{4}$ cup soft bread crumbs and $\frac{1}{4}$ cup shredded sharp process American cheese. Sprinkle over lobster mixture in shells. Bake at 350° for 20 minutes. Trim each serving with a sprig of parsley and serve with lemon wedges, if desired. Makes 4 servings.

Lobster Tails Maison

 8 small lobster tails, cut in thirds
 2 tablespoons butter or margarine
 2 teaspoons chopped shallots
 2 tablespoons lemon juice
 4 drops bottled hot pepper sauce
  Dash salt
 1 teaspoon bottled steak sauce
 ½ cup dry white wine
 1 cup whipping cream
 1 tablespoon butter or margarine,
  softened
 2 tablespoons all-purpose flour
 2 teaspoons chopped chives
   . . .
 ¼ cup whipping cream
 ½ cup hollandaise sauce
  Green grapes

In heavy skillet brown lobster tails in the 2 tablespoons butter. Add shallots; cook till tender but not brown. Add lemon juice, hot pepper sauce, salt, steak sauce, wine, and cream; heat to boiling. Combine the 1 tablespoon butter and flour; add to sauce. Add chives. Return sauce to boiling; simmer 2 to 3 minutes.

Fill 6 individual casserole dishes with ¼ cup of the sauce; arrange 4 pieces lobster along the outside edge. Whip the ¼ cup cream; blend together whipped cream and hollandaise sauce. Spread 2 tablespoons mixture over each filled dish. Garnish with green grapes. Broil 4 inches from heat for about *1 minute;* serve casseroles immediately. Makes 6 servings.

Lobster Supreme

 1 10-ounce package frozen
  artichoke hearts
 1 bay leaf
 1 tablespoon chopped onion
 1 teaspoon butter or margarine
   . . .
 1 10½-ounce can condensed
  cream of mushroom soup
 ½ cup light cream
 2 tablespoons dry sherry
 2 ounces sharp process American
  cheese, shredded (½ cup)
 1 5-ounce can lobster, drained
  and broken in large pieces
  Hot cooked rice

Cook artichoke hearts with bay leaf as directed on package in *unsalted* water. Drain; remove bay leaf. Cut artichoke hearts in half. In skillet or blazer pan of chafing dish cook onion in butter till tender but not brown. Add soup, cream, and wine, stirring till smooth. Add cheese; heat and stir till melted.

Add artichoke hearts and lobster; heat through. Keep warm in skillet or over hot water. Serve over fluffy hot rice. Serves 4.

Lobster Stew

 ¼ cup butter or margarine
 2 6-ounce lobster tails, cooked
  and cut in bite-sized pieces
 2 cups light cream
 1 cup milk
 1 teaspoon salt
 ¼ teaspoon Worcestershire sauce
  Dash bottled hot pepper sauce

In large saucepan melt butter; add lobster and cook 5 minutes. Add cream, milk, seasonings, and dash pepper; heat to scalding. Remove from heat; cover and let stand 15 minutes to blend flavors. If necessary, reheat to serving temperature. Ladle into heated soup dishes. If desired, float a dot of butter atop each serving and garnish with paprika. Serves 4.

Float a pat of butter on top of individual bowls of Lobster Stew. This creamy, New England recipe boasts peppy seasonings.

Lobster-Cheese Waffles

An extraordinary combination—

2 tablespoons butter or margarine
2 tablespoons all-purpose flour
¼ teaspoon salt
1½ cups milk

. . .

2 ounces sharp process American
   cheese, shredded (½ cup)
1 5-ounce can lobster, drained,
   flaked, and cartilage removed
1 teaspoon lemon juice

. . .

Cheese Waffles

In a saucepan melt butter or margarine. Blend in all-purpose flour and salt. Add milk. Cook and stir mixture till thickened and bubbly. Remove from heat. Add shredded cheese; stir till melted. Stir in lobster and lemon juice. Reheat just to boiling. Serve over hot Cheese Waffles. Makes about 4 servings.

Cheese Waffles: Sift together 1¼ cups sifted all-purpose flour; 2 teaspoons baking powder, 1 teaspoon sugar, and ¼ teaspoon salt. Stir in 2 ounces sharp process American cheese, shredded (½ cup). Combine 1 beaten egg, 1¼ cups milk, and ¼ cup salad oil; add to dry ingredients, mixing only till dry ingredients are moistened. Bake in preheated waffle baker.

Lobster Salad

Serve in avocado boats—

1 5-ounce can lobster, drained
   and flaked
2 tablespoons lemon juice
¾ cup sliced celery
⅓ cup mayonnaise or salad dressing
¼ teaspoon salt
   Dash pepper
2 avocados, peeled and halved
   lengthwise
   Lemon juice

Sprinkle flaked lobster with 2 tablespoons lemon juice. Add sliced celery, mayonnaise or salad dressing, salt, and pepper. Mix lightly; chill thoroughly. Brush the avocados with lemon juice; mound the chilled lobster salad atop avocado halves. Makes 4 servings.

Lobster-Orange Cups

1 5-ounce can lobster, drained
   and cartilage removed

. . .

¼ teaspoon salt
3 large oranges, peeled and
   sectioned
2 tablespoons mayonnaise or
   salad dressing
¼ teaspoon grated orange peel
2 tablespoons orange juice
¼ teaspoon prepared horseradish

. . .

½ cup whipping cream

Break lobster into ½-inch pieces; sprinkle with salt. Toss with orange sections. Chill. To prepare dressing combine mayonnaise or salad dressing, orange peel, orange juice, and horseradish. Whip cream; gently fold into mayonnaise mixture.

Heap chilled lobster-orange mixture in individual lettuce-lined bowls or sherbet glasses. Pass whipped cream dressing. Top with dash of nutmeg, if desired. Makes 3 or 4 servings.

Lobster Ring Mold

An elegant main dish salad—

1 envelope unflavored gelatin
   (1 tablespoon)
¾ cup milk
1 cup dairy sour cream
2 tablespoons tarragon vinegar
½ teaspoon onion salt
1 5-ounce can lobster, drained,
   flaked, and cartilage removed
1 8-ounce carton cream-style
   cottage cheese
½ cup diced peeled cucumber
⅓ cup sliced celery

In a saucepan heat the unflavored gelatin in milk; stir over low heat till the gelatin is completely dissolved. Cool thoroughly.

Beat in dairy sour cream, tarragon vinegar, onion salt, and ½ teaspoon salt till smooth. Chill till partially set. Fold in flaked lobster, cream-style cottage cheese, diced cucumber, and sliced celery. Pour into 4½-cup ring mold. Chill till firm. Makes 4 servings.

LOGANBERRY—A purplish red berry thought to be a natural cross between the blackberry and the red raspberry. This berry, named for a Judge Logan of California who discovered it, resembles the blackberry in shape and the raspberry in color and flavor.

Because fresh loganberries perish quickly, only canned loganberries are available in most parts of the country. Like other berries, loganberries may be used in a variety of desserts, salads, and beverages including wine. (See also *Berry*.)

LOIN—The long section of tender meat which follows the backbone between the shoulder and the round in a meat animal. Rib chops and roasts, T-bone steaks, and sirloin roasts and steaks are among the retail cuts from the loin. (See also *Meat*.)

LOMILOMI SALMON (*lō' mē lō' mē*)—A Hawaiian salad made of salmon and fresh vegetables. (See also *Hawaiian Cookery*.)

LONDON BROIL—A broiled beef steak, generally flank. Before broiling, the steak is scored and marinated. (See also *Beef*.)

London Broil

Diagonal carving is the secret to success—

1 1½-pound top-quality beef
    flank steak
    . . .
1 cup salad oil
1 tablespoon vinegar
1 small clove garlic, minced
    Salt
    Pepper

Score flank steak. Place in shallow pan. In mixing bowl combine salad oil, vinegar, and minced garlic; pour over steak. Cover; let stand at room temperature 2 to 3 hours, turning several times. Remove meat from marinade, draining thoroughly. Place steak on cold rack in broiler pan. Broil, 3 inches from heat, about 5 minutes; season with salt and pepper. Turn; broil 5 minutes more (for medium-rare); season. To serve, carve in very thin slices diagonally across grain. Makes 4 or 5 servings.

LOQUAT (*lō' kwot, kwat*)—The small, yellow to orange fruit of an evergreen tree that is native to Japan and eastern Asia. The loquat tree, also called the Japanese medlar, is often grown for its decorativeness as well as for its fruit.

The loquat has a thin, downy skin, pale yellow to orange flesh, and several large black seeds. The fruit's slightly tart flavor has been likened to that of a cherry.

Although in recent years the cultivation of this subtropical fruit has moved into areas such as Florida, California, and several of the Gulf States, the loquat is still, not widely known or readily available in the United States. It is occasionally available in specialty food stores.

Loquats are delicious eaten fresh or used in desserts, jellies, or preserves.

LORD BALTIMORE CAKE—A tall, yellow layer cake filled with a mixture of frosting, macaroons, maraschino cherries, and chopped nuts, then generously frosted with fluffy white frosting. This elegant cake was probably named for an early Maryland settler known as Lord Baltimore.

LOUIS (*Loo'ē*)—A tomato-flavored salad dressing served with seafood, particularly crab. (See also *Crab Louis*.)

LOUP DE MER—A variety of sea bass. (See also *Sea Bass*.)

LOVAGE (*luv' ij*)—A leafy herb which resembles celery in both appearance and flavor. This relative of parsley and celery is a native of southern Europe or Asia.

The lovage plant, which grows up to seven feet tall, has light to dark green leaves and a large stalk. The root is sometimes used as a cooked vegetable or candied. The lovage leaves are the part of the plant usually used for seasoning.

The ancient Greeks and Romans used lovage as a seasoning and also chewed it as a digestive aid. Former generations also believed this herb to be an aid to circulation and a treatment for rheumatism.

Fresh or dried lovage leaves add a delightful celerylike flavor to salads, soups, sauces, stews, casseroles, poultry stuffing, and tea. (See also *Herb*.)

LOW-CALORIE COOKERY

Tips on how to maintain a good-looking figure, plus a guide for planning low-calorie menus.

What to do about keeping that bulge from appearing around your stomach is a problem that confronts many people today. Do you go on a crash diet, starve away the pounds, visit a doctor, or use a diet?

Included in this article are a number of low-calorie cookery tips that offer the overweight individual a sensible approach to weight control through the use of food preparation techniques that help keep calories at a minimum and/or the use of commercial low-calorie ingredients.

Many of these overweight problems stem from the high standard of living most of us enjoy today. What we haven't learned to do is balance this standard of living against our calorie needs. For example, the early-day farmer required approximately 1500 *more* calories per day than does the average twentieth-century American man. But then he was out in the fields all day hoeing, raking, and walking acres behind a horse. The same was true of the pioneer homemaker, who did not have a washing machine, gas or electric range, vacuum sweeper, or the other labor-saving devices available to the modern woman. She needed 1000 *more* calories per day than does the modern American woman.

The problem, then, is how to enjoy this standard of living and still maintain a trim figure. First, you must accept that far too

A slimming main dish

←A jiffy low-calorie entrée—Italian-Sauced Fish—is easy to prepare with canned spaghetti sauce and shredded mozzarella cheese.

many people eat too much. Second, you have to recognize that few of us take part in enough physical exercise. To control your weight, you have to understand what calories are and what they do for you.

Food furnishes calories which are units of heat energy used by the body. These calories (units of energy) are required to perform continuous body functions: circulation, digestion, and elimination. Calories also provide the energy needed by the body to perform physical activities.

To perform all these functions, your body needs just so many calories. Any excess is stored in the body. Consume a few more calories than your body burns and you'll gain a little weight. Consume many more calories than you need and you'll get fat.

How do you know how many calories you need for each day? Your daily weight is, of course, a good guide. If you maintain a good figure, you're probably controlling your weight properly. During infancy, adolescence, pregnancy, and lactation, the body requires more calories than at any other time. After the body has passed the growing stage—normally around age 21— fewer calories are needed to keep the body functioning properly. Also, when you cease any serious physical activity, your body needs fewer calories.

Coupled with growth and development is a person's basic physical size. Larger people usually require a bigger daily calorie intake, for the higher proportion of muscle tissue to fat tissue increases the body's need for calories. Likewise, your sex is another essential factor to consider. Save for times of pregnancy, women generally require fewer calories than do men.

Taking into consideration the above mentioned factors concerning calorie needs, certain statistics will hold true for most people who are trying to maintain the proper weight. Approximately 3500 calories equal 1 pound of fat body tissue. Cut your daily intake by 500 calories and you'll lower your weight by 1 pound per week. Double this figure and you reach the maximum week loss recommended by doctors.

However, before undertaking any weight-loss program, consult your doctor. He will tell you what you can safely do. With this knowledge and the daily recommended calorie intake for you (see box above), you can work out your own low-calorie program.

Frequently, overweight people go on a crash diet program to get down to the desired weight. But what happens when the crash diet is over and you're back to your normal calorie intake? Up goes your weight and once again your tipping the scales.

Preparing food

Many foods are relatively low in calories—at least initially. Whether or not their calorie counts soar or maintain the desired level depends on the techniques you use when preparing them. So, if your calorie intake is limited, it is vital that you use low-calorie cooking methods.

Appetizers: To prepare low-calorie snacks or hors d'oeuvres, marinate bite-sized appetizers, such as shrimp, Brussels sprouts, or artichoke hearts in low-calorie salad dressing. For a low-calorie dip, blend cottage cheese, Neufchâtel cheese, or low-calorie mayonnaise-type dressing with herbs. Serve with vegetable dippers—carrot or celery sticks, cherry tomatoes, and cauliflowerets. For a first course appetizer, select a fresh fruit cup and pour a low-calorie carbonated beverage over fruit.

Marinated Sprouts

Cook one 10-ounce package frozen Brussels sprouts following package directions; drain. Halve large pieces. Mix ½ cup low-calorie Italian salad dressing; 1 small clove garlic, minced; 2 tablespoons finely chopped onion; 1 teaspoon dried parsley flakes; and ½ teaspoon dried dillweed. Pour over sprouts. Cover; marinate in refrigerator several hours. Drain; pass cocktail picks. Makes 2 cups.

Party Cheese Dip

    1 5-ounce jar Neufchâtel
        cheese spread with pimiento
    1 cup dry cottage cheese
    3 tablespoons skim milk
    1 teaspoon prepared horseradish
        Several drops bottled hot
            pepper sauce

Combine all ingredients; beat till thoroughly blended and fluffy. Chill. Serve with raw vegetables or cooked shrimp. Makes 1¼ cups.

Zesty Zucchini Dip

In a saucepan combine 2 cups diced zucchini (2 medium); 1 tablespoon chopped onion; ½ cup tomato juice; ½ teaspoon salt; and ⅛ teaspoon basil leaves, crushed. Simmer, covered, for 20 minutes. Put mixture in blender container; add one 8-ounce package Neufchâtel cheese, cubed. Cover; blend on high speed till smooth. Remove from blender; chill. Before serving, stir in 1 tablespoon bacon-flavored bits. Makes about 1⅔ cups.

Tomato Refresher

Combine 2½ cups tomato juice, 3 tablespoons lemon juice, ⅛ teaspoon celery salt, 1 teaspoon Worcestershire sauce, and noncaloric sweetener equal to 1 teaspoon sugar; chill. Stir before serving. Top each serving with a paper-thin lemon slice. Makes 5 servings.

Green and Gold Compote

    1 20-ounce can dietetic-pack
       pineapple chunks
    2 small fully ripe bananas
    3 oranges
    ½ pound seedless green grapes
    1 cup low-calorie lemon-lime
       carbonated beverage, chilled

Drain pineapple, reserving liquid. Slice bananas on the bias into reserved liquid; drain. Peel and slice oranges; remove seeds. Halve orange slices. Wash grapes; divide in small clusters. In bowl layer pineapple, bananas, and oranges. Mound grapes in center. Chill. Before serving, slowly pour chilled carbonated beverage over fruit. Makes 5 cups.

Appropriate as an appetizer, a salad, or a dessert, Green and Gold Compote features a bountiful display of fruit low in calories.

Main dishes: Protein-rich foods, such as meat, poultry, fish, cheese, and eggs, contribute a major proportion of the calories in a weight control program. The calorie content of these foods, however, is kept at a minimum when low calorie cooking techniques are used. For example, fewer calories are present when meat is trimmed of excess fat or when poultry is skinned before cooking. Likewise, meats prepared by broiling or roasting are lower in calories than when fat is added, as in deep-fat frying.

For meat dishes prepared in a skillet, use a nonstick pan. Begin cooking the meat at a low temperature to allow some of the meat juices to collect in the pan, thus eliminating the need for adding fat. If gravy is prepared from the meat juices, skim off excess fat before thickening.

Fish and seafood are generally lower in calories than is meat or poultry. If fish is prepared by broiling, brush occasionally with fruit juice or low-calorie salad dressing to keep fish moist during cooking.

To reduce calories in main dish sandwiches, eliminate the second slice of bread and serve sandwiches open-face. Also use softened butter or margarine for spreading bread as it spreads more easily and less is needed than when butter is firm.

Turkey-Cheese Sandwich

    1 10-ounce package frozen
       asparagus spears
    2 tablespoons chopped onion
    ½ cup low-calorie Italian salad
       dressing
    3 tablespoons low-calorie
       mayonnaise-type dressing
    4 slices white bread, toasted
    8 1-ounce slices cooked turkey
    4 slices process Swiss cheese,
       halved diagonally (4 ounces)

Cook asparagus following package directions; drain. Mix onion, salad dressing, and ¼ teaspoon pepper; pour over spears in saucepan. Bring to boiling; remove from heat. Spread mayonnaise-type dressing on toast. Top *each* with 2 slices of turkey, several hot spears, and 2 triangles of cheese. Broil 5 inches from heat till cheese melts, 2 to 3 minutes. Serves 4.

Ham Barbecue

½ cup catsup
2 tablespoons chopped onion
1 tablespoon Worcestershire sauce
2 teaspoons lemon juice
2 teaspoons prepared mustard
¼ teaspoon chili powder
　Noncaloric liquid sweetener
　　equal to 1 tablespoon sugar
1 fully cooked ham slice
　(1½ pounds)

Combine first 7 ingredients. Slash fat edge of ham at 2-inch intervals. Brush meat liberally with sauce; let stand 1 hour. Broil 3 to 4 inches from heat 5 to 6 minutes per side, turning once and brushing with sauce. Serves 8.

Curried Chicken Breasts

Skin, bone, and halve lengthwise 3 broiler-fryer chicken breasts (2 pounds). Sprinkle with ½ teaspoon seasoned salt and dash paprika; place in 11x7x1½-inch baking pan. In a small saucepan drain liquid from one 3-ounce can sliced mushrooms; add 1 chicken bouillon cube. Heat and stir till bouillon is dissolved.

To saucepan add sliced mushrooms, ¼ cup dry sauterne, ½ teaspoon instant minced onion, ¼ teaspoon curry powder, and dash pepper; pour over chicken. Cover with foil; bake at 350° for 40 minutes. Uncover and bake 20 minutes longer. Serve with pan juices. Serves 6.

Italian-Sauced Fish

2 16-ounce packages frozen
　flounder fillets, thawed
1 8-ounce can spaghetti sauce
　with mushrooms
2 tablespoons chopped onion
1 4-ounce package shredded
　mozzarella cheese (1 cup)

Arrange the fillets in a single layer on a well-greased 15½x10½x1-inch baking sheet. Sprinkle with salt. Mix spaghetti sauce and onion; pour over fillets. Bake, uncovered, at 350° till fish flakes easily with fork, 25 to 30 minutes. Sprinkle with cheese; return to oven till cheese melts, about 3 minutes. Serves 8.

Pampered Beef Fillets

1 3-ounce can chopped mushrooms,
　drained
¼ cup snipped green onion
1 cup red Burgundy
9 4-ounce beef fillets
　(1 inch thick)
9 fresh mushroom crowns
　(optional)

In saucepan combine chopped mushrooms, onion, and ½ cup water; simmer 5 minutes. Stir in wine, 1 teaspoon salt, and dash pepper. Place fillets in plastic bag. Pour in wine sauce; fasten bag securely. Marinate in refrigerator several hours. Remove fillets, reserving sauce. Broil 3 inches from heat 7 minutes; turn and broil 6 minutes. During last few minutes, top with mushroom crowns (X-shaped slash in top). Sprinkle with snipped parsley, if desired. Heat sauce; spoon over fillets. Serves 9.

Vegetables and salads: Vegetables are excellent in low-calorie diets and are often included in unlimited amounts since they are generally low in calories, yet high in nutrients. For variety, offer raw as well as cooked vegetables in the diet. To serve cooked vegetables, sprinkle with lemon juice or season with herbs, for, if butter or margarine is added for seasoning, calories are quickly increased.

To reduce calories in creamed vegetables, prepare the white sauce using little or no fat. Blend the flour with a small amount of skim milk; then stir the flour mixture into the remaining milk. Bring the mixture to boiling and cook until it is thick and bubbly. Avoid serving rich sauces that overpower the vegetable in flavor.

Salads add nutrients and bulk to the diet without adding excessive calories. Whether it's a main dish, fruit, or vegetable salad, calories are controlled when a low-calorie salad dressing is used. If the salad dressing is made at home, use oil sparingly or toss salad ingredients with lemon juice or vinegar. Another calorie-saving idea is to thicken fruit or vegetable juices and blend them with herbs. Likewise, commercially prepared low-calorie salad dressings further aid the dieter when serving salad.

Sizzling Pampered Beef Fillets topped with mushroom crowns highlight a low-calorie meal. Assorted vegetables complete the menu.

Skillet Onion Slices

In skillet heat ¼ cup low-calorie Italian salad dressing, ⅓ cup water, and ½ teaspoon salt. Cut 3 large onions in ½-inch slices; place onion slices in single layer in skillet.

Cover; cook over low heat, 10 minutes. Turn; sprinkle with 2 tablespoons snipped parsley, 2 tablespoons shredded Parmesan cheese, and dash paprika. Cook, uncovered, 5 minutes longer. Makes 6 servings.

Basil-Carrot Coins

Slice 6 medium carrots. Simmer, covered, in salted water till tender, about 10 to 15 minutes. Drain carrots. Combine 1 tablespoon butter or margarine, melted; ¼ teaspoon salt; and ¼ teaspoon dried basil leaves, crushed; toss with carrots. Makes 6 servings.

Ruby-Sauced Beets

In saucepan blend 2 teaspoons cornstarch, 2 teaspoons sugar, and dash salt. Blend in ½ cup low-calorie cranberry juice cocktail; stir over medium heat till thickened and bubbly. Add one 16-ounce can sliced beets, drained, and ¼ teaspoon shredded orange peel. Simmer, uncovered, for 10 minutes. Makes 4 servings.

Cabbage Aspic

  2 envelopes unflavored gelatin
    (2 tablespoons)
  4 cups tomato juice
  ½ medium onion, sliced
  3 stalks celery, 3 inches long
  2 lemon slices
  2 bay leaves
    Noncaloric liquid sweetener
      equal to 2 tablespoons sugar
  2 teaspoons prepared horseradish
  2 cups chopped cabbage *or* 1 cup
    chopped celery

Soften gelatin in ½ *cup* tomato juice; set aside. In saucepan combine remaining tomato juice, onion, celery stalks, lemon, and bay leaves. Bring to boiling; reduce heat and simmer, covered, for 10 minutes. Strain. Add softened gelatin to tomato mixture. Return to low heat and stir till gelatin is dissolved. Stir in noncaloric sweetener, horseradish, ½ teaspoon salt, and dash pepper. Chill till partially set. Fold in cabbage. Pour into eight ½-cup molds. Chill till firm. Makes 8 servings.

Tuna Salad in Iceberg Ring

  1 ⅞-ounce package low-calorie
    lime-flavored gelatin
    (2 envelopes)
  ½ teaspoon salt
  2 tablespoons vinegar
  3 cups coarsely chopped iceberg
    lettuce
  ¼ cup thinly sliced green onion
    Tuna Salad

Dissolve gelatin and salt in 2 cups boiling water. Stir in 1½ cups cold water and vinegar. Chill till partially set. Fold in lettuce and onion. Pour into 5½-cup ring mold. Chill till firm, about 3 hours. To serve, unmold ring. Fill center with Tuna Salad. Serves 6.

Tuna Salad: Combine ½ cup low-calorie mayonnaise-type dressing, 2 tablespoons capers, 1 tablespoon lemon juice, ¼ teaspoon salt, and dash pepper; set aside. Drain two 6½-ounce cans water-pack tuna, chilled; break in pieces. Combine tuna and ¾ cup diced cucumber. Just before serving, toss tuna-cucumber mixture with dressing mixture.

A light and refreshing summertime salad, Tuna Salad in Iceberg Ring, is geared to the weight watcher. For variety, serve other meat salads in the colorful lettuce-filled lime mold.

Cottage Cheese Dressing

In blender container combine 1 cup cottage cheese, not creamed; noncaloric liquid sweetener equal to 2 tablespoons sugar; and 4 teaspoons lemon juice. Blend till creamy. Using about ½ cup skim milk, add 1 tablespoon at a time, till of desired consistency. Makes 1 cup.

Slim-Trim Dressing

Mix 1 tablespoon cornstarch and ½ teaspoon dry mustard. Stir in 1 cup water. Cook and stir till thick; cool. Add ¼ cup vinegar; ¼ cup catsup; ½ teaspoon *each* paprika, prepared horseradish, and Worcestershire sauce; dash noncaloric sweetener; and dash salt. Beat. Add 1 clove garlic, halved; chill. Makes 1⅓ cups.

Desserts: Though many desserts are traditionally high in calories, a variety of low-calorie desserts are possible using low-calorie cooking techniques and/or commercial low-calorie dessert products. Low-calorie desserts may include fruit cups, compotes, ices, puddings, and chiffons.

To prepare fruit desserts, use fresh fruit or purchase fruit packed in its own juice. For refrigerated desserts using whipped cream, calories are reduced when whipped evaporated skim milk is substituted for the whipping cream. Likewise, custards and puddings are lower in calories when made with skim milk rather than whole milk.

Although desserts are often served with whipped cream or ice cream, a fruit garnish, a sprinkling of ground spice, or a low-calorie whipped topping is equally attractive.

Baked Custard

3 slightly beaten eggs
2 cups skim milk, scalded
½ to 1 teaspoon vanilla
   Noncaloric liquid sweetener
      equal to ¼ cup sugar

Mix eggs and ¼ teaspoon salt. Stir in cooled milk, vanilla, and sweetener. Fill six 6-ounce custard cups; set in shallow pan on oven rack. Pour hot water into pan, 1 inch deep. Bake at 325° till knife inserted off-center comes out clean, 40 to 45 minutes. Serves 6.

Coffee Chiffon

Soften 2 envelopes unflavored gelatin (2 tablespoons) in ½ cup cold water. In saucepan beat 2½ cups skim milk and 3 egg yolks. Add noncaloric liquid sweetener equal to ½ cup sugar, 1 tablespoon instant coffee powder, ½ teaspoon salt, and gelatin. Cook and stir till gelatin dissolves and mixture thickens. Chill till partially set. Beat 3 egg whites, 1 teaspoon vanilla, and ¼ teaspoon cream of tartar till soft peaks form. Fold in gelatin. Spoon into 6½-cup mold. Chill until firm. Makes 10 servings.

Planning menus

Whether you maintain weight by counting calories or merely by eating less food, you must balance your diet nutritionally. To do this, each day's menus should provide the number of servings recommended by the Basic Four. To check this, use the Basic Four Menu Guide for planning your menus. Select foods from each group which are relatively low in calories. However, if your caloric allotment is quite low, it is not always possible to include the total number of bread servings.

To plan a lunch or dinner menu, select a main dish from the Meat Group that provides one serving for each family member. Add a vegetable, salad, bread, dessert, and beverage that complement the main dish.

By planning menus in advance, a wider variety of foods is possible, and you are assured of a sound weight control program. Remember, however, that serving portions must be controlled for an effective program.

Basic four menu guide

Milk Group—2 to 4 cups daily

Includes milk, buttermilk, yogurt, ice cream, and cheese.
   Recommended allowances:
      2 to 3 cups for children
      4 or more cups for teen-agers
      2 or more cups for adults
   Calcium equivalents for 1 cup milk:
      1⅓ ounces Cheddar-type cheese
      1½ cups cottage cheese
         1 pint (2 cups) ice cream

Meat Group—2 servings daily

Includes beef, veal, pork, lamb, poultry, fish, and eggs. Alternate sources of protein which may be used occasionally include dry beans, dry peas, dry lentils, nuts, and peanut butter.
   Consider as one serving:
      2 to 3 ounces of cooked meat, fish,
         or poultry
      2 eggs
      1 cup cooked dry beans, peas, or lentils
      4 tablespoons peanut butter

Vegetable-Fruit Group—4 servings daily

Include one serving of citrus fruit or tomato daily and one serving of a dark green leafy vegetable, deep yellow vegetable, or yellow fruit 3 to 4 times a week. Use other fruits and vegetables for the remaining servings
   Consider as one serving:
      ½ cup fruit or vegetable
         1 medium apple, banana, or potato
      ½ grapefruit or cantaloupe

Bread-Cereal Group—4 servings daily

Includes breads, cereals, cornmeal, grits, crackers, rice, quick breads, macaroni, noodles, spaghetti, and other pasta products. These products should be made from whole grain, enriched, or restored cereals.
   Consider as one serving:
      1 slice bread
      ¾ to 1 cup ready-to-eat cereal
      ½ to ¾ cup cooked cereal, rice, macaroni,
         noodles, or spaghetti

MENU

1000 CALORIES

BREAKFAST—204 calories
½ cup Fresh Strawberries
1 cup Crisp Rice Cereal
½ cup Skim Milk   1 teaspoon Sugar
Coffee or Tea

LUNCH—360 calories
3 ounces lean Broiled Ground Beef Patty
½ Hamburger Bun
1 teaspoon Catsup or Mustard
1 cup Lettuce
1 tablespoon low-cal
Blue Cheese Salad Dressing
Lemon-Blueberry Fluff
½ cup Skim Milk   Coffee or Tea

DINNER—448 calories
Seafood Divan
½ cup Cottage Cheese
½ medium Fresh Peach on Lettuce Leaf
Grapefruit-Berry Compote
1 cup Skim Milk   Coffee or Tea

Seafood Divan

Cook two 10-ounce packages frozen broccoli spears following package directions; drain. Arrange in greased 11¾x7½x1¾-inch baking dish. Toss one 5-ounce can lobster, drained and flaked, with one 4½-ounce can shrimp, drained and deveined; spoon over broccoli.

In shaker mix ¼ cup skim milk, 2 tablespoons all-purpose flour, and ¼ teaspoon salt; shake well. Combine flour mixture, 1¼ cups skim milk, and 1 tablespoon butter. Cook and stir till mixture is thick and bubbly; reduce heat. Add 2 ounces process Swiss cheese, shredded (½ cup); stir to melt. Pour over seafood, covering seafood; sprinkle with paprika. Bake at 400° for 20 to 25 minutes. Makes about 8 servings.

Grapefruit-Berry Compote

1 10-ounce package frozen raspberries
2 tablespoons sugar
3 inches stick cinnamon
½ teaspoon whole cloves
2 large white grapefruit

Thaw berries; drain, reserving syrup. Mix syrup, ¼ cup water, sugar, cinnamon, and cloves; bring to boiling. Reduce heat. Simmer, uncovered, 10 minutes; strain. Peel and section grapefruit; place in 10x6x1¾-inch baking dish. Top with berries; pour syrup over fruits. Cover; chill several hours. Serves 6.

Lemon-Blueberry Fluff

1 3-ounce package lemon-flavored gelatin
1 cup boiling water
¼ teaspoon grated lemon peel
2 tablespoons lemon juice
¾ cup cold water
2 egg whites
1 9-ounce carton frozen unsweetened blueberries, thawed
1 tablespoon cornstarch
2 tablespoons sugar
Few drops vanilla

Dissolve gelatin in 1 cup boiling water. Stir in peel, juice, and ¾ cup cold water. Chill till partially set. Add unbeaten egg whites to gelatin mixture. Beat with electric mixer till light and fluffy, 1 to 2 minutes. Pour into eight 5-ounce custard cups. Chill till firm. (Slight separation into layers may occur.)

In saucepan crush ½ *cup* of the berries. Blend cornstarch with ½ cup cold water. Add cornstarch mixture and sugar to crushed berries. Cook and stir over medium heat till thick and bubbly; cook and stir 1 minute more. Remove from heat; stir in remaining berries and vanilla. Chill. To serve, unmold desserts in individual dishes. Top with sauce. Serves 8.

An elegant ending

Lemon-Blueberry Fluff is an excellent dessert for entertaining. What's more, guests will never suspect you're counting calories.

MENU

1200 CALORIES

BREAKFAST—230 calories
½ Grapefruit
½ cup Puffed Wheat Cereal
½ cup Skim Milk   1 teaspoon Sugar
1 Poached Egg
Coffee or Tea

LUNCH—384 calories
Cottage-Shrimp Toss
4 Crisp Rye Crackers
¼ medium Cantaloupe
1 cup Skim Milk   Coffee or Tea

DINNER—578 calories
Stuffed Cube Steak
Baked-Stuffed Potato
1 cup Lettuce   1 small Tomato
1 tablespoon low-cal
Italian Salad Dressing
Ambrosia Delight
1 cup Skim Milk   Coffee or Tea

Cottage-Shrimp Toss

6 cups torn Boston or bibb lettuce
1 tablespoon salad oil
1 tablespoon wine vinegar
2 7-ounce packages frozen
   shrimp in shells, cooked,
   peeled, and cleaned
1 12-ounce carton cream-style
   cottage cheese (1½ cups)
¼ cup coarsely chopped dill pickle
2 tablespoons sliced green onion

In bowl sprinkle lettuce with salt and pepper
toss with oil and vinegar. Reserve a few whole
shrimp; coarsely chop remaining shrimp. Toss
chopped shrimp and remaining ingredients with
lettuce. Garnish with whole shrimp. Serves 6

Stuffed Cube Steaks

6 beef cube steaks (1¾ pounds)
½ cup low-calorie French-style
   salad dressing
1 cup shredded carrot
¾ cup finely chopped onion
¾ cup finely chopped green pepper
¾ cup finely chopped celery
½ cup canned beef broth
4 teaspoons cornstarch
¼ teaspoon Kitchen Bouquet

Pound steaks to ¼-inch thickness. Sprinkle generously with salt and pepper; brush with salad dressing. Place in shallow dish; marinate 30 to 60 minutes at room temperature.

In saucepan combine carrot, onion, green pepper, celery, ¼ cup water, and ¼ teaspoon salt. Simmer, covered, till crisp-tender, 7 to 8 minutes. Drain. Place ⅓ cup vegetable mixture on each steak. Roll up jelly-roll fashion; secure with wooden picks. Place rolls in 10-inch skillet; pour broth over. Simmer, covered, till tender 35 to 40 minutes.

Transfer meat to serving platter; remove picks. Skim fat from broth; reserve ¾ cup broth. Blend cornstarch with 2 tablespoons cold water; stir into reserved broth. Cook and stir till thick and bubbly; stir in Kitchen Bouquet. Pour over steak rolls. Serves 6.

Baked-Stuffed Potatoes

Scrub 3 medium baking potatoes; puncture skin with fork; bake at 425° for 1 hour. Cut potatoes in half lengthwise. Scoop out inside; mash. Combine ⅓ cup hot water, 3 tablespoons nonfat dry milk powder, ½ teaspoon salt *or* imitation butter-flavored salt, and dash pepper. Add to potatoes; beat till fluffy, adding additional hot water if needed. Pile lightly into shells; sprinkle with paprika. Return to oven till hot, about 10 minutes. Serves 6.

Ambrosia Delight

Peel and section 4 medium oranges over bowl to catch juices. To oranges and juice add 2 ripe medium bananas, sliced, and 3 maraschino cherries, quartered. Toss. Sprinkle with 2 tablespoons shredded coconut. Serves 6.

MENU

1500 CALORIES

BREAKFAST—334 calories

¼ medium Honeydew Melon

1 Blueberry Muffin

1 slice Broiled Bacon

1 cup Skim Milk   Coffee or Tea

LUNCH—541 calories

½ cup Creamed Chipped Beef on 1 Rusk

1 cup Lettuce   1 small Tomato

1 tablespoon low-cal
French-Style Salad Dressing

Baked Orange Cup

1 cup Skim Milk   Coffee or Tea

DINNER—641 calories

Deviled Steak

½ cup Scalloped Potatoes

⅔ cup Broccoli

Cucumber Salad

1 slice French Bread

Lime Snow   2 Vanilla Wafers

Coffee or Tea

2 teaspoons butter or margarine
allowed for the day

Baked Orange Cups

Using sharp knife, remove tops of 4 medium oranges. With grapefruit knife, scoop out pulp and reserve. Set orange shells aside. Dice reserved orange pulp; toss with ½ cup seedless green grapes, halved, and dash bitters.

Spoon fruit mixture into orange shells. Place in 10x6x1¾-inch baking dish. Pour a little water around fruit-filled orange shells. Bake at 325° for 25 minutes. Sprinkle with 2 tablespoons flaked coconut. Bake 8 to 10 minutes longer. Makes 4 servings.

Deviled Steak

Trim excess fat from 1½ pounds beef sirloin steak, cut 1 inch thick. Broil steak 3 inches from heat, 5 to 6 minutes on each side; steak will be rare. In skillet combine 2 tablespoons butter, 1 tablespoon snipped parsley, 1 tablespoon dry sherry, 1 teaspoon dry mustard, 1 teaspoon Worcestershire sauce, ¼ teaspoon salt, and dash pepper; heat till bubbly.

Add steak. Pour 2 tablespoons warm brandy over steak; flame. When brandy has burned down, remove steak. To skillet add ¼ cup catsup and one 4-ounce can sliced mushrooms, drained; mix well. Serve on steak. Serves 6.

Cucumber Salad

Peel 1 large cucumber; halve lengthwise and remove seeds. Slice cucumber into blender container; cover. Blend on high speed till puréed. Stop blender, as needed, to push cucumber down from side of container. Add water to purée, if necessary, to make 1 cup.

Mix 1 envelope unflavored gelatin (1 tablespoon) and 2 tablespoons sugar; add 1 cup unsweetened pineapple juice. Stir over low heat till gelatin and sugar dissolve. Add cucumber, 4 teaspoons lemon juice, and 1 to 2 drops yellow food coloring. Chill till partially set; stir occasionally. Pour into 3½-cup mold. Chill till firm. Pass *Yogurt Dressing:* Mix ¼ cup plain yogurt, 1 tablespoon low-calorie mayonnaise-type dressing, 1½ teaspoons sugar, and ½ teaspoon lemon juice. Chill. Serves 4.

Lime Snow

In saucepan combine 1 envelope unflavored gelatin (1 tablespoon); ⅓ cup sugar, and ¼ teaspoon salt. Stir in 1¼ cups cold water. Stir over low heat till gelatin is dissolved.

Remove from heat. Add one 6-ounce can frozen limeade concentrate and ½ teaspoon grated lemon peel; stir to thaw. Chill till partially set. Turn into large bowl; add 2 unbeaten egg whites and 2 to 3 drops green food coloring. Beat at high speed with electric mixer till light and fluffy, 1 to 2 minutes.

Pour into 5½-cup mold or eight 5-ounce custard cups. Chill till firm. (Slight separation may occur.) Makes about 8 servings.

LOW FAT MILK—Milk that has less milk fat than does whole milk. Although any skim milk (fat content less than 0.5 percent) can be classified as low fat milk, low fat is most commonly used in connection with milk having a fat content of about 2 percent compared to about 3½ percent fat content in whole milk. (See *Milk, Skim Milk* for additional information.)

LOX—Fresh salmon fillets that are halved and cured, then lightly smoked. Although widely used by central Europeans, lox is most often associated with Jewish people.

Lox is always served cold. With cream cheese and a toasted bagel, it is the Jewish breakfast deluxe. Lox accompanied by capers is also frequently served at buffets.

LUAU (*lōō ou′, lōō′ ou*)—A Hawaiian feast. These gala occasions with a more than ample supply of food, a festive spirit, and lively entertainment epitomize the friendly atmosphere of the Hawaiian Islands.

Originally, luaus were held by Hawaiian settlers as thanksgiving feasts. Later on, however, a luau was considered a part of the celebration at weddings, engagements, births, and other important occasions. Today, the luau is a celebration in itself and needs no special occasion.

As with any other feast, food is one of the essential ingredients at a luau. At a traditional luau, the foods served are typically Hawaiian—*poi* (taro root paste), *haupia* (coconut pudding), edible seaweed, pineapples, papayas, and many other tropical fruits. All of these foods are eaten with the fingers.

The traditional main dish is a whole pig roasted in an underground oven (imu). This oven consists of a pit heated with hot stones and lined with ti leaves. The cavity of the whole pig is filled with hot stones after which the animal is lowered into the oven. After surrounding the meat with a variety of tropical fruits and vegetables, such as bananas, breadfruit, and sweet potatoes, the oven is covered with ti leaves or burlap and then earth.

Lively entertainment is the second essential luau ingredient. Islanders playing soothing, body swaying music, hula dancers, and other native dancers are typically Hawaiian, thus adding much to the tropical atmosphere of the luau. Everyone's fun is greatly increased if they participate actively in the dancing and singing.

The decorations at a luau also add much to the festive mood of this feast. Greenery and bright tropical flowers are used in abundance. Often, a long, low table is completely covered with leaves on which exotic flowers such as orchids and hibiscus are scattered. Sometimes, leaves are even used as serving plates and bowls. Since luaus are usually held outdoors, the surrounding area and its greenery contribute to the atmosphere. Part of the magic of the decorations is that, surrounded by all of this beauty, guests will completely relax and enjoy themselves a great deal.

In recent years, mainlanders and other tourists in Hawaii have become so intrigued by this form of hospitality that they have begun staging their own luaus at home. Even though many of the tropical foods and decorations are not available in the continental United States, the luau is successful as long as the festive mood and essential hospitality are maintained. (See also *Hawaiian Cookery*.)

LUNCH BOX LUNCH—A fairly light meal packed in a portable carrier. Many homemakers find that they not only have to pack a daily lunch box lunch for the youngsters to take to school but also for the teen-age son to take to his part-time job and for the man of the house to take to the office. Providing an attractive meal is often a challenge to the housewife. Included here are some appealing lunch box ideas that will help overcome this challenge.

Buy ready-to-travel foods, such as cakes, breads, cheeses, potato chips, pickles, crackers, and even canned puddings, in serving-sized packages. Complement the lunch box foods with a can of frozen vegetable or fruit juice. It will be thawed but still cold at lunchtime. Use a vacuum bottle to carry either hot or cold beverages. Fresh fruit wrapped in clear plastic wrap is an easy dessert to pack. To make peeling an orange easier, cut the peel in sections and pull back one end of each. If dessert is a frosted cupcake, invert a paper cup over the cake to protect the frosting.

Lunch Box Menus

Main Dish or Sandwich	Salad or Vegetable	Dessert	Beverage
Chili Con Carne* Crackers	Tossed Vegetable Salad with French Dressing	Scotch Shortbread*	Milk
Vegetable-Beef Soup* Crackers	Mixed Fruit Salad	Cake Brownies*	Orange Drink
Cheese Chowder* Melba Toast	Whole Apple	Everyday Cupcake*	Tomato Juice
Chilled Asparagus Soup* Sesame Seed Crackers	Nectarine	Fruitcake	Spiced Tea*
Old Time Beef Stew* Hard Roll	Celery Sticks Olives	Red Cherry Pie*	Lemonade*
Wiener-Bean Bake* Boston Brown Bread	Pineapple-Carrot Toss*	Peanut Butter Cupcakes*	Coffee
Club Sandwich*	Orange Olives and Pickles	Jelly Roll* Slice	Breakfast Cocoa*
Corned Beef on Rye with Dill Pickles	Coleslaw*	Peach Pie*	Raspberry Cooler*
Sliced Ham on Whole Wheat Hard-cooked Egg	Tomato Slices	Chocolate Pudding	Iced Tea
Roast Beef Sandwich* Potato Chips	Mustard Beans*	Ripe Plum	Eggnog*
Submarine Sandwich*	Applesauce	Date Pudding Cake*	Carbonated Beverage
Swiss Cheese on English Muffin	Raw Cauliflowerets Pickles	Gingerbread*	Grape Juice
Bacon-Peanut Butter Sandwich	Carrot Sticks Radishes	Apricot Foldovers*	Hot Mulled Cider*
Chef's Salad Bowl* Raisin-Cinnamon Rolls*		Pecan Crispies*	Chocolate Malted Milk
Cottage Cheese Best Nut Loaf*	Mixed Fruit Salad Shawano Dressing*	Gumdrop Gems*	Hot Tea

All starred recipes appear in these encyclopedias. See index for page numbers.

Sandwiches are by far the most frequent lunch box food. Save yourself time by making a week's supply of sandwiches at once, wrapping each separately or placing in sandwich bags, then storing them in the freezer. Sandwich fillings that freeze well include peanut butter, chicken, and meat. Pack these sandwiches while they are frozen, and they will be just right for lunch.

To vary the sandwiches a little, use a variety of breads, such as white, rye, whole wheat, and nut breads and perk up the sandwich with fresh lettuce and tomato packed individually. These vegetables will stay fresher if wrapped separately in foil or clear plastic wrap and then added to the sandwich at lunchtime.

The introduction of wide-mouth vacuum containers, which keep hot foods hot and cold foods cold, has definitely broadened the variety of foods that can be packed in the lunch box. Use them for chilled mayonnaise mixtures, such as potato and chicken salads, chilled puddings and custards, gelatin salads, and canned fruits, as well as hot soups and casseroles. The handy wide mouth makes it possible to spoon the food out of the container.

Although packing lunches sometimes seems a very tedious chore, the family is sure to appreciate your efforts if you take time to add the little extras.

LUNCHEON MEAT—A subtly spiced, canned, pressed meat product made from pork with beef sometimes added. Although luncheon meat is fully cooked when purchased, many people prefer to heat it before serving.

Fruited Luncheon Loaf

    2 12-ounce cans luncheon meat
    1 11-ounce can mandarin oranges,
       drained
    1 22-ounce can raisin pie filling
    2 tablespoons vinegar

Cut *each* loaf of luncheon meat lengthwise in 8 slices to within 1 inch of bottom. Arrange mandarin oranges between meat slices. Place loaves in shallow baking pan; bake at 375° for 20 minutes. Heat raisin pie filling with vinegar. Serve with meat. Makes 8 servings.

Frosted Luncheon Meat

Anchor canned luncheon meat on a spit. Blend 2 parts pasteurized process cheese spread and 1 part Dijon-style prepared mustard; spread on all sides of luncheon meat. Broil over *hot* coals till golden brown. Slice and serve on toasted buns. Pass remaining sauce.

Meat and Yam Skillet

    1 12-ounce can luncheon meat, cut
       in 8 slices
    Whole cloves
    1 tablespoon butter or margarine
              . . .
    1 16-ounce can sweet potatoes,
       drained
    Salt
    ⅓ cup peach *or* pineapple preserves

Stud luncheon meat with whole cloves. In skillet brown meat on both sides in butter or margarine; push to one side of skillet.

Add sweet potatoes; sprinkle sweet potatoes with salt. Spoon preserves over meat and potatoes. Heat, uncovered, over low heat; baste mixture often till meat and potatoes are hot and glazed, about 5 minutes. Makes 4 servings.

Skillet Barbecue

    ½ cup chopped onion
    2 tablespoons butter or margarine
              . . .
    1 cup catsup
    ⅓ cup water
    ¼ cup brown sugar
    3 tablespoons vinegar
    1 tablespoon prepared mustard
    1 tablespoon Worcestershire sauce
    1 12-ounce can luncheon meat, cut
       in julienne strips
              . . .
    Hot cooked rice *or* toasted
       hamburger buns

Cook onion in butter or margarine till tender but not brown. Stir in catsup, water, brown sugar, vinegar, mustard, Worcestershire sauce, and luncheon meat. Simmer, uncovered, 15 minutes. Serve over rice or on buns. Serves 6.

Speedy Kabobs

Brushed with a flavorful tomato sauce—

1 13½-ounce can pineapple chunks
1 8-ounce can tomato sauce
¼ cup finely chopped green onion
¼ cup butter or margarine
1 teaspoon Worcestershire sauce

. . .

1 12-ounce can luncheon meat
1 green pepper, cut in 12 squares
2 medium tomatoes, quartered

Drain pineapple chunks, reserving ½ cup syrup. To make sauce combine tomato sauce, reserved syrup, finely chopped green onion, butter or margarine, and Worcestershire sauce in saucepan. Simmer till thick, about 15 minutes.

Cut luncheon meat into 12 cubes. On four 9-inch skewers, alternately thread pineapple chunks, meat chunks, and green pepper squares; brush with sauce. Broil kabobs 5 to 6 inches from heat till browned, about 8 to 9 minutes. Turn; add quartered tomatoes to skewers. Brush thoroughly with sauce; broil till browned, about 4 to 5 minutes more. Makes 4 servings.

Macaroni-Meat Skillet

An easy-to-fix main dish—

1 cup chopped celery
½ cup chopped onion
1 clove garlic, minced
2 tablespoons shortening
1 12-ounce can luncheon meat,
   cut in sticks

. . .

1 10¾-ounce can condensed tomato
   soup
½ 7-ounce package macaroni
1½ cups water
⅛ teaspoon pepper

In large skillet or saucepan cook chopped celery, chopped onion, and minced garlic in hot shortening till tender but not brown. Add luncheon meat sticks; brown lightly.

Stir in condensed tomato soup, uncooked macaroni, water, and pepper. Bring to boil; reduce heat. Cover. Cook 25 minutes, stirring occasionally. Makes 4 to 6 servings.

Broiled Luncheon Meat Sandwiches

4 ounces sharp process American
   cheese, shredded (1 cup)
3 tablespoons mayonnaise or salad
   dressing
2 tablespoons chopped green onion

. . .

6 slices bread, toasted
Prepared mustard
1 12-ounce can luncheon meat, cut
   in 12 thin slices

Combine shredded cheese, mayonnaise or salad dressing, and chopped green onion. Lightly spread toasted bread with mustard; top each bread slice with 2 slices luncheon meat. Spread with cheese mixture. Broil 4 inches from heat till cheese melts, about 3 minutes. Makes 6.

Mandarin Roasts

1 11-ounce can mandarin oranges
½ cup honey
2 tablespoons finely chopped
   candied ginger
2 to 3 tablespoons lemon juice
2 or 3 12-ounce cans luncheon meat

Drain mandarin oranges, reserving ¼ cup syrup. Combine reserved syrup, honey, and candied ginger. Bring to boiling and cook 5 minutes. Add lemon juice and orange sections.

Cut each loaf of luncheon meat on the diagonal to make 2 wedges. Grill over *hot* coals 30 minutes, turning occasionally, and brushing the last 15 minutes with the orange sauce. To serve, garnish meat with a few of the orange sections (tack with wooden picks); heat remaining sauce to pass. Makes 4 to 6 servings.

LUTEFISK *(lōōd' uh fisk, lōōt')*—A Scandinavian dish made of fish that were soaked in a solution of lye and water during processing. (See also *Scandinavian Cookery*.)

LYONNAISE-STYLE *(lī' uh nāz')*—A technique of preparing foods with sautéed onions. This technique originated in Lyons, France. Foods prepared lyonnaise-style are usually vegetables, particularly potatoes.

M

MACADAMIA NUT (*mak' uh dā' mē uh*)—
A small, two-kernel nut with a flavor resembling that of an almond. Macadamia trees are apparently native to Australia although they are little known there today.

The world's primary producer of this nut is the Hawaiian Islands, where macadamia trees were introduced in the 1880s and first cultivated commercially in the early 1900s. At first, many farmers felt that macadamia nuts were an unprofitable crop because the trees require 18 years to produce the nuts. However, the demand for this exotic nut coupled with the development of steam rollers to crack the extremely tough nutshell convinced islanders to plant macadamia groves. Although the supply still has not caught up with the demand, increasingly more macadamia nuts are being harvested each year in Hawaii.

Like other nuts, macadamia nuts are high in fat, but they also contain small amounts of protein, vitamins, and minerals. Six whole, roasted macadamia nuts contribute about 110 calories to the diet.

The most popular use for this tasty nut, available shelled and canned as both whole nuts and pieces, is as a cocktail accompaniment. However, macadamia nuts are an ingredient in many Hawaiian dishes, and they are delicious in a variety of salads, confections, main dishes, pies, cakes, cookies, and other desserts. (See also *Nut*.)

Macadamia Nut Pie

Reminiscent of pecan pie—

In mixing bowl blend together ¼ cup sifted all-purpose flour, 2 tablespoons sugar, and ¼ teaspoon salt. Stir in 1 cup light corn syrup and 1 cup honey. Combine 4 slightly beaten eggs, ½ teaspoon vanilla, and 3 tablespoons butter or margarine, melted; stir into syrup mixture. Pour filling mixture into 1 *unbaked* 9-inch pastry shell (See *Pastry*). Sprinkle with ¾ cup coarsely broken macadamia nuts.

Bake at 350° till knife inserted halfway between center and edge of pie comes out clean, about 55 to 60 minutes. Cool. If desired, whip ½ cup whipping cream and spoon onto pie.

Peaked Pineapple Salad

Macadamia nuts add crunch—

Combine 2 cups melon balls; 1 cup sliced pitted dates; 2 medium bananas, peeled and sliced; and ¼ cup chopped macadamia nuts. Whip 1 cup whipping cream with 2 tablespoons sugar, 1 tablespoon lemon juice, and dash salt till soft peaks form. Fold into fruit mixture. Drain one 20½-ounce can pineapple slices, chilled. Line 10 salad plates with lettuce; arrange one pineapple slice atop lettuce on *each* plate. Pile fruit mixture over. Makes 10 servings.

MACARONI—Tubelike pasta. Macaroni's basic ingredients are flour (usually semolina, a granulation made of durum wheat) and water. Named according to shape, macaroni varieties are so numerous that they span the alphabet from *acini di pep* to *ziti*.

Macaroni, like pasta, is an Italian word, so we tend to think of macaroni as having originated in Italy. Certain history books support this view as does the Spaghetti Museum located in Pontedassio, Italy. On display there are documents such as Papal bulls regulating the quality of pasta dating back to the thirteenth century. However, it was during this same century that Marco Polo made his journeys to the Orient, and some historians tell us that he brought pasta to Italy from there. Still others contend that this food came to Germany via the invading Mongols in the thirteenth century and spread from there to Italy. Some documents, on the other hand, record that pasta was eaten as early as 5000 B.C.

Although it is difficult to make a very strong case for any of these theories, the Italians unquestionably deserve the credit for developing macaroni into most of its present intricate forms.

Place of origin has little to do with the present-day enjoyment of macaroni. Its popularity rests more upon its many attributes. Heading the list of these is its versatility. Since it is bland in flavor, macaroni is a good base in recipes ranging from the garlic-laden creations of the Provence region of France to the cinnamon-spiced pastitsio of Greece. Economy is another factor that assures a place for macaroni among the staples of all income levels, as is the fact that refrigerator storage is not required before cooking.

How macaroni is made: The manufacture of macaroni begins by kneading semolina and water into a smooth dough. This dough is then forced through a die (pierced metal plate). A pin centered in each opening in the die results in a tube shape as the dough passes through. Each macaroni variation has its own special die. If a curved shape such as the "elbow" is to be produced, a notched pin is used. This allows the dough to move through the die more quickly on one side than the other, producing a curled effect. When "alphabets" are made, a letter-shaped die is used, and the dough is cut very short. After the macaroni is shaped, it is dried, depending on the variety, in drying ovens or cabinets by slowly passing filtered air over it.

Nutritional value: It is always good news when a food we enjoy is good for us, too. Such is the case with macaroni. A two-ounce serving of enriched macaroni provides the following percentages of the daily allowances: 25 percent of the thiamine, 12 percent of the riboflavin, 20 percent of the niacin, and 16 percent of the iron.

A one-cup serving of enriched macaroni provides about 9 percent of the protein needed daily and adds just 155 calories to the day's count. The sauce that tops the macaroni will add a good many more calories, but macaroni dishes "stick to the ribs" and so lessen the need for calorie-laden between-meal snacks.

Types and kinds: The creation of the myriad shapes of macaroni has been a feat of artistry and imagination. This array, including stars, wheels, and spirals, not only provides variety but also inspires the cook to create kitchen masterpieces.

Macaroni Shells Florentine features macaroni shells filled with spinach-cottage cheese and baked in a Parmesan sauce.

Spoon up hearty servings of Macaroni and Cheese for Saturday lunch. The delectable combination of sharp American cheese and elbow macaroni is sure to make this dish a family favorite.

There are as many macaroni sizes and shapes as there are recipes using it. Starting with the smallest, here are a few examples of macaroni types:
1. Small shapes: Anellini (tiny rings), conchigliette (little conch shells), and tripolini (little bows) are all good soup ingredients as are the children's favorite soup ingredient, "alphabets."
2. Medium sizes: Americans are best acquainted with the elbow style, but a number of other shapes are also available. Tortiglione (twists), rote (wheels), and farfalle (butterflies) are just a few of the varieties that are available.
3. Large varieties: Manicotti (small muffs), conchiglioni (jumbo conch shells), and rigatoni (large grooves) are

a sampling from a long list of types of macaroni that are usually served with a stuffing of some sort.

How to select and store: Which macaroni you choose depends on the recipe to be prepared. However, if a particular type is not available, simply substitute another macaroni of similar size. If the opened package can be tightly resealed, use it to store the uncooked macaroni. Otherwise, transfer the macaroni to a storage container with a tight-fitting cover. Uncooked macaroni doesn't need refrigerating but it should be stored in a cool place.

Once cooked, macaroni can be stored in the refrigerator for a day or two, or for as long as six months in the freezer.

How to prepare: When you are cooking macaroni, remember that using a generous amount of vigorously boiling water is the key to success. You'll need a large saucepan because two quarts of water are needed for each half-pound of macaroni cooked. Also, watch carefully to make sure the macaroni does not cook too long. Then, add two tablespoons of salt to give the macaroni flavor. If you put a little cooking oil in the water, this will reduce splashing and prevent the surface of the cooked macaroni from drying out.

Boil macaroni until it reaches a stage Italians call "al dente" (to the tooth), which means it is still slightly chewy. There should be no trace of starchy flavor as this is an indication that the macaroni is underdone. Just how many minutes it takes to reach "al dente" is a much-debated topic among pasta experts, but most of them agree that taste tests should begin after the macaroni has boiled for eight minutes. Small macaroni types take less time to cook than do the larger types.

How to use: When using macaroni in a dish that requires further cooking, cut the boiling time by one-third to avoid overdone macaroni. When using macaroni in soup, prevent it from becoming overly soft by adding it to the other ingredients no more than 15 minutes before serving.

Macaroni is frequently served with a sauce. Great care and imagination have gone into the creation of appropriate toppings. Often meat, fish, or cheese is the main ingredient, and vegetables, herbs, and spices are used to complete the sauce.

It is best to cook macaroni at serving time, but occasionally this is inconvenient. If you must cook it ahead, drain the macaroni well and hold it briefly under cold running water. Drain again and cover. At serving time return the macaroni to boiling water just long enough to bring it back to serving temperature. (See also *Pasta*.)

Macaroni and Cheese

Cook 1½ cups elbow macaroni in boiling, salted water till tender; drain. In saucepan melt 3 tablespoons butter or margarine; blend in 2 tablespoons all-purpose flour, ½ teaspoon salt, and dash pepper. Add 2 cups milk; cook and stir till thickened and bubbly. Add ¼ cup finely chopped onion (optional) and 8 ounces sharp process American cheese, cubed (2 cups); cook and stir till cheese is melted.

Mix cheese sauce with cooked macaroni. Turn into 1½-quart casserole. Sprinkle 1 medium tomato, sliced, with salt; arrange atop macaroni. Bake at 350° 35 to 40 minutes. Serves 6.

Macaroni vocabulary

Because many Italian terms are associated with macaroni, a few definitions may be helpful.

Zuppa or *in brodo* indicates a soup recipe. The macaroni called for in this category are usually delicate and add to the eye appeal as well as to the nourishment of the dish. *Minestra* refers to both soup and first course. *Minestrone*, that well-known vegetable soup made with macaroni, is substantial enough to make a meal in itself.

Macaroni *bollita* simply means boiled macaroni. This pasta is generally served with some type of zesty sauce.

Macaroni *imbottita* is stuffed macaroni. A flavorful mixture goes inside and a sauce generally goes on top.

Al forno means baked macaroni. Many of our best beloved pasta casseroles, such as lasagne, are of this type.

Cheddar–Macaroni Bake

4 ounces corkscrew macaroni
    (1½ cups)
¼ cup sliced pimiento-stuffed
    green olives
2 tablespoons all-purpose flour
¼ teaspoon dry mustard
¼ teaspoon salt
    Dash pepper
1¾ cups milk
6 ounces sharp process American
    cheese, shredded (1½ cups)
½ teaspoon Worcestershire sauce
1 cup soft bread crumbs
2 tablespoons melted butter

Cook macaroni in boiling, salted water; drain. Combine with olives, flour, mustard, salt, and pepper. Turn into 1 quart casserole.

Combine milk, shredded cheese, and Worcestershire sauce. Heat till cheese melts. Pour over macaroni mixture. Combine bread crumbs and melted butter. Sprinkle atop casserole. Bake at 350° till hot, about 40 minutes. Serves 4.

Easy Mexican Skillet eliminates cooking the macaroni separately. Simply simmer the macaroni in the flavorful sauce till done.

Macaroni Omelet

¼ cup elbow macaroni
4 egg yolks
¼ cup shredded sharp process
    American cheese
4 stiffly beaten egg whites
2 tablespoons butter or margarine
    Creole Sauce

Cook macaroni in boiling, salted water till tender; drain. Beat egg yolks and dash salt till thick and lemon-colored; stir in macaroni and cheese. Fold in egg whites. Melt butter in 10-inch skillet; when hot, pour in omelet mixture. Cook over low heat 8 minutes. Finish cooking at 325° till lightly browned. Loosen with spatula. Make shallow cut across center of omelet; fold in half. Remove to hot platter; serve with Creole Sauce. Serves 4 to 6.

Creole Sauce: Cook 3 tablespoons finely chopped onion and 3 tablespoons finely chopped green pepper in 2 tablespoons butter or margarine till tender but not brown. Add one 8-ounce can tomato sauce, one 3-ounce can broiled chopped mushrooms with liquid, and dash pepper. Simmer, uncovered, 10 minutes, stirring occasionally. Makes about 1⅓ cups.

Sausage Macaroni and Cheese

1 pound bulk pork sausage
½ cup chopped onion
1 cup uncooked elbow macaroni
1 10½-ounce can condensed cream of
    celery soup
⅔ cup milk
3 slightly beaten eggs
1 cup shredded sharp process
    cheese
¾ cup corn flakes, crushed
1 tablespoon butter or margarine,
    melted

Cook sausage and onion till meat is lightly browned; drain off excess fat. Cook macaroni according to package directions; drain.

Combine sausage mixture, drained macaroni, cream of celery soup, milk, eggs, and shredded cheese. Place in an 8x8x2-inch baking dish.

Mix corn flake crumbs and melted butter or margarine; arrange in border. Bake at 350° for 40 minutes. Makes about 6 servings.

Macaroni Shells Florentine

Filled with a savory spinach mixture—

  20 jumbo macaroni shells (about
       7 ounces)
          . . .
  ½ cup chopped celery
  2 tablespoons chopped onion
  2 tablespoons cooking oil
  2 cups cream-style cottage cheese
  1 10-ounce package frozen chopped
       spinach, cooked and drained
  1 slightly beaten egg
  ½ teaspoon salt
  ⅛ teaspoon dried oregano leaves,
       crushed
  ⅛ teaspoon ground nutmeg
     Dash pepper
     Cheese Sauce

Cook macaroni shell according to package directions; drain. Cook celery and onion in hot oil till tender but not brown; drain. Combine onion mixture, cottage cheese, cooked spinach, egg, salt, oregano, nutmeg, and pepper; mix well. Fill shells with spinach mixture.

Pour *half* the Cheese Sauce into 12x7x2-inch baking dish. Arrange stuffed macaroni shells in sauce. Bake, covered, at 375° for 15 minutes. Drizzle on remaining Cheese Sauce. Bake, uncovered, 10 minutes more. Serves 8 to 10.

Cheese Sauce: In saucepan cook 2 tablespoons chopped onion in 3 tablespoons cooking oil; blend in 3 tablespoons all-purpose flour, ¼ teaspoon salt, and dash pepper. Stir in 1½ cups milk and ¾ cup chicken broth. Cook and stir till the sauce is thickened and bubbly. Stir in ¼ cup grated Parmesan cheese.

Easy Mexican Skillet

In skillet lightly brown 1 pound bulk pork sausage; drain off excess fat. Add ½ cup chopped green pepper and ¼ cup chopped onion; cook till tender. Stir in one 16-ounce can tomatoes, one 8-ounce can tomato sauce, 1 cup uncooked elbow macaroni, 2 tablespoons sugar, 1 teaspoon salt, and 1 teaspoon chili powder. Cover and simmer for about 20 minutes.

Stir in ½ cup dairy sour cream; heat mixture through, but do not let it boil. Pass grated Parmesan cheese. Makes 5 servings.

Chewy Coconut Macaroons toasted to a golden brown are the perfect finish to a large meal. Serve them with a scoop of sherbet.

MACAROON—A small, meringue-based cookie characterized by a crisp outer crust and a chewy interior. Today, these delightful cookies are often made with shredded or flaked coconut instead of the traditional almond paste or ground almonds. Since these cookies harden when they are stored, the best time to eat them is when they are fresh. (See also *Cookie.*)

Coconut Macaroons

An easy-to-make delicacy—

  2 egg whites
     Dash salt
  ½ teaspoon vanilla
  ⅔ cup sugar
  1 3½-ounce can flaked coconut
       (1⅓ cups)

Beat egg whites with salt and vanilla till soft peaks form. Gradually add sugar, beating till stiff peaks form. Fold in flaked coconut.

Drop by rounded teaspoon onto a greased baking sheet. Bake at 325° for about 20 minutes. Makes about 1½ dozen macaroons.

For easy-to-remove macaroons

Forget the traditional, yet often troublesome paper-lined baking sheet and use a greased cookie sheet for macaroons. When cooled slightly after baking, the macaroons are easy to remove from the cookie sheet.

Macaroons

> 1 8-ounce can almond paste
> 1 cup granulated sugar
> 3 egg whites
> 1/3 cup sifted confectioners' sugar
> 2 tablespoons flour
> 1/8 teaspoon salt

In small mixer bowl crumble almond paste; gradually beat in granulated sugar and egg whites. Mix together confectioners' sugar, flour, and salt; blend into almond paste-sugar mixture. Drop by teaspoonfuls onto greased cookie sheet or press through pastry bag, using large rose point. Bake at 300° till lightly browned, about 25 minutes. Let stand one or two minutes before removing from pan. Makes about 32.

MACE—The lacy, fibrous covering of a nutmeg. When dried, mace is used as a spice. Mace and nutmeg, often called "sister spices," are the only two common spices that come from the same tree. Although fresh mace is crimson in color, during drying, this spice changes to the golden yellow to orange color familiar to the homemaker. Mace is so light that it takes hundreds of nutmegs to yield one pound of mace.

Mace, a native of the Spice Islands, was not familiar in Europe as early as some of the other spices, such as cinnamon. During the Middle Ages, spice trade increased and mace became one of the most prized spices. Had you lived during the thirteenth century, it would have cost you three sheep to purchase a pound of mace.

Through the centuries, the main growing area for this spice was the Far East and today, this area (particularly Indonesia) still provides a large majority of the mace imported to the United States.

The homemaker will find ground mace readily available on the supermarket spice shelf and in some areas, whole mace, called blades, is also available.

Like its sister, nutmeg, mace has numerous cooking uses. A blade of mace subtly flavors fish sauces, jellies, preserves, pickles, and Welsh rarebit. However, for many dishes ground mace is more appropriate than are blades. In yellow cakes, this spice contributes color as well as flavor. Mace and chocolate are flavorful partners in cakes, pies, and other desserts.

Also, a little ground mace is delicious used in fish and seafood stews, fruit salads and desserts, baked goods, puddings, custards, cooked vegetables such as carrots and spinach, whipped cream, and meat loaves. Once you have become familiar with this delightful spice, you're sure to find many other uses for it. (See also *Spice*.)

Lemon-Mace Rounds

These are delicately spicy—

> 2 cups sifted all-purpose flour
> 2 teaspoons baking powder
> 1/2 teaspoon salt
> 1/4 teaspoon ground mace
> 2 eggs
> 3/4 cup granulated sugar
> 2/3 cup salad oil
> 1/4 cup brown sugar
> 2 teaspoons grated lemon peel
> 2 teaspoons lemon juice
> 1/4 cup granulated sugar
> 1/2 teaspoon ground nutmeg
> 1/4 teaspoon ground mace

Sift flour, baking powder, salt, and 1/4 teaspoon mace together. Combine eggs, 3/4 cup granulated sugar, salad oil, brown sugar, lemon peel, and lemon juice; beat until thick. Stir in dry ingredients. Drop by teaspoon about 2 inches apart on lightly greased cookie sheet.

In small mixing bowl combine 1/4 cup granulated sugar, nutmeg, and 1/4 teaspoon mace. Lightly butter bottom of glass; dip in sugar and spice mixture and press cookies flat. Bake at 400° till lightly browned, about 8 minutes. Makes about 3 dozen cookies.

MACÉDOINE *(mas' i dwän')*—The French word for a mixture of fruits or vegetables cut in pieces of uniform size. A fruit macédoine, usually made of either raw or cooked fresh fruit that is in season, is most frequently served as an appetizer, salad, or dessert. Vegetable macédoines are usually made of cooked vegetables and may be served either hot or cold.

MACERATE *(mas' uh rāt')*—To soak foods in a liquid to soften them and to absorb flavor. Macerate and marinate mean essentially the same thing, but macerate is usually applied to fruits and vegetables, while marinate is applied primarily to meats.

MACKEREL—A saltwater fish that lives in both the Atlantic and Pacific oceans. Today, the mackerel is one of the most important food fish in the United States, just as it was in the days of the early colonists. In fact, during colonial times, fishing seasons for mackerel were established.

Mackerel belong to the *Scombridae* family. Other members of this family include the bonito, Spanish mackerel, and king mackerel. The bonito is a strong-flavored fish that is caught mainly in the summer and fall months. The Spanish mackerel is also a strong-flavored, yet tasty fish, and it is probably the most expensive of all the mackerels. It is caught off the Florida coast during the winter months. The king mackerel is larger than the Spanish mackerel and, in addition to having a fine flavor, it is a good game fish.

General characteristics of the mackerel include a deep blue back marked with wavy lines and a silvery underside. This fish usually measures from 12 to 18 inches in length. Mackerel is a fat fish with a very rich flavor. The flesh is quite firm and is usually red. Since it is a fat fish, mackerel is best baked or broiled.

Mackerel can be purchased canned, frozen, fresh, salted, and smoked. The salted mackerel is best if soaked before using.

Nutritionally, mackerel is a source of protein, vitamin A, and the B vitamins, thiamine, niacin, and riboflavin. Canned mackerel also contains some calcium. One broiled fillet of mackerel equals about 300 calories and a half cup of canned mackerel equals 192 calories. A 3½-ounce portion of salted mackerel has 305 calories, while the same portion of smoked mackerel equals 219 calories. (See also *Fish.*)

MADELEINE *(mad' uh lin)*—A small, French tea cake baked in a special scalloped mold.

MADRAS TEA *(mad' ruhs, muh dras')*—Black tea produced in and named for a province in southern India. (See also *Tea.*)

MADRILÉNE *(mad' ruh len', län')*—A term applied to dishes flavored with tomatoes. Madrilene, literally meaning "in the style of Madrid," is most commonly applied to a tomato-flavored consommé.

Chicken Madrilene

A special chilled soup—

    1 envelope unflavored gelatin
        (1 tablespoon)
    1 cup chilled tomato juice
    2 chicken bouillon cubes
    1½ cups water
        Dash pepper
    2 tablespoons dry sherry
            . . .
        Chopped chives
        Lemon wedges

Soften unflavored gelatin in *half* of the tomato juice. In a saucepan heat bouillon cubes and water to boiling, stirring to dissolve. Add the softened gelatin. Stir till gelatin is dissolved. Add the remaining tomato juice, pepper, and the two tablespoons of dry sherry.

Chill, stirring 2 or 3 times, till partially set. Then chill till firm. Spoon into serving dishes. Trim with chopped chives and serve with lemon wedges. Makes 4 to 6 servings.

MAGNESIUM—A mineral, concentrated in the bones and teeth, that is essential for the proper functioning of the body. Numerous common foods such as spinach, walnuts, and peanut butter contain magnesium.

MAGNUM—A large wine bottle that holds approximately two quarts.

MAHIMAHI *(mä′ hē mä′ hē)*—The Hawaiian or Polynesian word for dolphin. Mahimahi is found in tropical waters and is usually sold to restaurants in large fillets which are then cut into serving-sized pieces. The flesh of this mammal is delicately flavored. (See also *Hawaiian Cookery*.)

MAID OF HONOR—A rich English tea tart filled with lemon curd, jam, or another sweet filling. Richmond, a London suburb, is particularly famous for its delectable maids of honor. (See also *English Cookery*.)

MAIGRE *(mä′ guhr)*—The French word for lean. This word is sometimes applied to thin soups that do not contain any meat fat.

MAITRE D'HOTEL *(mä′ tuhr dō tel′, mä′ truh)*—The person in charge of the dining room. In the United States, this term is often shortened to maitre d'.

MAITRE D'HOTEL BUTTER—A sauce made by combining butter, parsley, and lemon juice. It is most commonly served with fish or grilled meats, such as steaks.

MALLARD DUCK—A wild duck characterized by glossy green to black throat feathers and a white ring around the neck. The majority of wild ducks shot by hunters are mallard ducks. (See also *Duck*.)

MALT—Germinated grain used in brewing, distilling, and for flavoring other foods. Compared to ungerminated grain, malted grain is sweeter, has a more wrinkled appearance, and contains more enzymes. Malt can be made from any grain, but barley is the grain most commonly used for this purpose.

Grain is changed to malt during a carefully controlled process that involves soaking the grain in water to start germination, then drying the grain to stop germination at the desired time. During the malting process, a number of enzymes are formed, and part of the starch in the grain is converted by the enzymes to sugar.

The primary use for malt is in beer brewing where it is responsible for much of the characteristic beer flavor. Malt is also used commercially for flavoring vinegar and in distilled alcohol. In the manufacture of distilled alcohol, the malt enzymes, which convert starch to sugar, are important rather than the malt flavor.

Even though homemakers do not usually use malt for brewing or distilling, they do use malted milk powder and malted cereal. In both these products, the malt contributes a delightful flavor. This flavor is used in a wide range of dishes.

Malted Oatmeal Bars

½ cup butter or margarine
1 cup sugar
2 eggs
1 teaspoon vanilla
½ cup sifted all-purpose flour
½ cup chocolate-flavored malted-milk powder
¾ cup quick-cooking rolled oats
½ cup chopped walnuts

In mixing bowl cream butter or margarine and sugar. Add eggs and vanilla. Beat well. Sift together flour, chocolate-flavored malted-milk powder, and ¼ teaspoon salt. Add to creamed mixture; mix well. Stir in rolled oats and chopped walnuts. Spread in greased 9x9x2-inch baking pan. Bake at 350° for 35 minutes. Cool. Cut in bars. Makes about 2 dozen.

Orange Crunch Muffins

2 cups sifted all-purpose flour
⅓ cup sugar
1 teaspoon baking powder
½ teaspoon baking soda
½ cup malted cereal nuggets
2 well-beaten eggs
1 tablespoon grated orange peel
1 cup orange juice
⅓ cup salad oil

In mixing bowl sift together sifted all-purpose flour, sugar, baking powder, ¾ teaspoon salt, and baking soda. Stir in malted cereal nuggets. Combine well-beaten eggs, grated orange peel, orange juice, and salad oil. Add all at once to dry ingredients, stirring just till moistened. Fill greased muffin pans ⅔ full. Bake at 400° for 20 to 25 minutes. Makes 14 to 16.

Chocolate Malted Cheesecake

1 cup sifted all-purpose flour
1/3 cup chocolate malted-milk
    powder
1/4 teaspoon baking powder
1/4 teaspoon salt
6 tablespoons butter or margarine
2 tablespoons sugar

. . .

1 8-ounce package cream cheese,
    softened
1 cup small curd cream-style
    cottage cheese
1/2 cup sugar
2 eggs
2 teaspoons vanilla
2 tablespoons all-purpose flour
1 cup milk
    Blanched whole almonds
      (optional)
    Unsweetened or semisweet
      chocolate (optional)

To make crust: Sift together the 1 cup flour, malted-milk powder, baking powder, and salt. Cream together butter or margarine and the 2 tablespoons sugar till light and fluffy. Blend malt mixture into creamed mixture. Set aside 1/4 cup crumb mixture. Press remaining into bottom and 1 1/2 inches up side of *ungreased* 9-inch springform pan. Bake at 350° for 15 to 20 minutes. Bake the reserved 1/4 cup crumb mixture on baking sheet for 8 to 10 minutes. Cool crust and crumbs thoroughly.

To make filling: In mixer bowl cream together cream cheese and cottage cheese till smooth. Gradually add the 1/2 cup sugar, creaming well. Add the eggs and vanilla; beat at *low* speed of electric mixer just till blended. Stir in the 2 tablespoons flour. Add milk, blending till smooth. Pour into baked crust.

Bake at 350° till knife inserted just off-center comes out clean, 35 to 40 minutes. Top with reserved crumbs. Chill at least 4 hours. If desired, garnish with blanched whole almonds which have been dipped in melted unsweetened or semisweet chocolate. Serves 12 to 16.

MALTED MILK—1. A powder made of dried milk and malt. 2. A cold beverage made of milk, malted milk powder, and usually ice cream. (See also *Beverage.*)

Malted Milk

1 cup cold milk
1/4 cup canned chocolate syrup
2 tablespoons malted-milk powder
1 pint vanilla ice cream

Combine milk, chocolate syrup, and malted-milk powder. Add vanilla ice cream; mix just to blend. Makes 3 1/3 cups.

MALTOSE—The type of sugar found in malt and a few other foods. Maltose is also produced as an intermediate product of food digestion. (See also *Sugar.*)

MALT VINEGAR—A sour liquid obtained by fermenting barley malt. (See also *Vinegar.*)

MANDARIN ORANGE—A small, yellow to reddish orange, loose-skinned citrus fruit. This traditional Christmastime fruit is characteristically easier to peel and to section than are other varieties of oranges. This delectable citrus fruit grows on a small tree that is characterized by its slender branches and its lance-shaped leaves.

Thousands of years ago, mandarin oranges, as well as sweet oranges, were known in China. However, it wasn't until the early nineteenth century that cultivation of mandarin oranges in Europe was recorded. These oranges were first planted in the United States during the 1840s.

Nutritional value: Like other varieties of oranges, mandarin oranges' most significant nutritional contribution is vitamin C. A 3 1/2-ounce serving of canned mandarin oranges contains about 60 calories.

Types of mandarin oranges: The mandarin orange family includes several varieties including tangerine, temple, and satsuma. The tangerine is probably the best known of these. Tangerines are especially popular in Christmas gift baskets.

For many years, the flavorful temple orange has been particularly favored near the growing areas in Florida. In recent years, however, modern shipping methods have made this distinctive orange available in many other parts of the country.

The label on canned mandarin oranges usually does not specify which type of mandarin was used. However, since most of the canned mandarin oranges available in the United States are imported from Japan, satsuma oranges, the principal variety grown in that country, probably make up the bulk of canned mandarins sold.

How to select and store: Counting all the numerous varieties of mandarin oranges, the season for this fresh citrus fruit usually extends from November to May or June. Although the shape and skin color of the varieties differ slightly, there are two things to avoid when selecting any variety of fresh mandarin orange—a skin that is detached from the pulp and a blemished skin. Always store the fresh oranges in the refrigerator (preferably in the crisper).

How to use: Easy-to-peel, fresh mandarin oranges are especially suitable for lunch box meals and other pick up snacks. Alone or coupled with a mild cheese, these sweet oranges make a quick and delicious dessert. Also combine fresh mandarin oranges with other fresh and canned fruits for delicious fruit salads, fruit cups, and compotes.

Canned mandarin oranges add a distinctive flavor to a variety of dishes. Perk up an appetizer fruit cup with the bright color and flavor of these miniature oranges. At your next outdoor barbecue, use mandarin oranges and meat cubes for a tasty kabob combination. And don't forget to use this delicious canned fruit in fruit salads, gelatin salads and desserts, ice cream sauces, and compotes. (See also *Orange*.)

Mandarin-Fig Whip

A quick-to-prepare dessert—

Prepare one 2-ounce package dessert topping mix according to package directions. Blend in one 8-ounce carton orange yogurt. Fold in one 11-ounce can mandarin orange sections, drained; 1 cup diced fig-filled cookies; and ¼ cup coarsely chopped walnuts.

Chill at least 3 to 4 hours. Stir just before serving to fluff up mixture. Pile lightly into sherbet glasses. Makes 6 servings.

Pork Mandarin

1½ pounds boneless lean pork, cut
   in 1-inch cubes
2 tablespoons salad oil
1 cup chicken broth*
1 11-ounce can mandarin orange
   sections (1⅓ cups)
¼ cup corn syrup
2 tablespoons soy sauce
2 tablespoons vinegar
2 tablespoons cornstarch
   . . .
1 tablespoon grated fresh gingerroot
   or 1 teaspoon ground ginger
1 small onion, thinly sliced and
   separated into rings
3 cups hot cooked rice

Brown meat on all sides in hot oil. Add the broth. Cover; simmer till tender, about 1 hour. Drain oranges, reserving syrup. Combine reserved orange syrup, corn syrup, soy sauce, and vinegar. Blend in cornstarch and ginger. Add sauce to meat with onion rings; cook and stir till the mixture thickens. Add oranges; heat through. Serve on bed of hot cooked rice. Makes 4 or 5 servings.

*Or use 1 chicken bouillon cube dissolved in 1 cup boiling water.

Mandarin-Pear Salad

Good salad when counting calories—

1 8-ounce carton yogurt
2 tablespoons sugar
2 tablespoons blue cheese,
   crumbled
5 fresh medium pears,
   cored, and halved
Leaf lettuce
2 11-ounce cans mandarin orange
   sections, chilled and drained

In small mixer bowl combine yogurt, sugar, and *1 tablespoon* of the crumbled blue cheese. Beat dressing mixture with rotary beater or electric mixer till smooth. Sprinkle dressing with remaining crumbled blue cheese.

Arrange pear halves on lettuce. Fill centers with mandarin orange sections. Pass blue cheese dressing. Makes 10 servings.

A pyramid of bright orange mandarin oranges serves as the background for this luscious Mandarin Soufflé (see *Citrus* for recipe).

MANDEL *(män'duhl)*—The German word for almond. (See also *Almond.*)

MANGO *(mańg' gō)*—A yellowish red, juicy tropical fruit with a large seed and a distinctive, spicy flavor.

Mangoes are associated with India in particular, where they were one of the first fruits cultivated. The early Indians were so fond of this fruit that they reportedly presented Buddha with a magnificent grove of mango trees.

It is unclear when mangoes were introduced to Europe and northern Africa where they are now common. But, by the early eighteenth century, this fruit was being cultivated in Brazil. From South America it was brought to the West Indies, Mexico, and eventually to Florida sometime during the nineteenth century.

Nutritional value: Vitamin A and iron are the most significant nutritional contributions of mangoes. An uncooked mango half provides almost all of the recommended daily allowance of Vitamin A and nearly 3 times the daily iron allowance, yet only a meager 66 calories.

How to select and store: The season for fresh mangoes extends from May to September. Although color is a guide to ripeness, ripe mangoes range from green to yellow and red depending on the variety, so use overall appearance rather than just color as the criteria for selection. Avoid mangoes that are soft or have more than just a few dark spots on the skin.

Since the mango is a tropical fruit, it is sensitive to cold temperatures. So, remember to store this fruit in a cool (about 50°), relatively humid place rather than in the refrigerator.

How to use: The most popular ways to serve this fresh fruit are whole as a pick up snack or sliced as a dessert. Mangoes are also delicious in fruit salads, fruit cups, ice cream, and combined with other ingredients in many other dishes.

In the major mango-growing areas, green mangoes are frequently canned or used to make preserves, chutney, sauces, and pickles. Some of these products are available in United States markets. (See also *Fruit.*)

Mangoes on the Half Shell

The unique flavor of this exotic fruit is at its best when you serve it this way—

With knife parallel to the long curved side of the chilled fruit, cut into mango at blossom end. Skim the knife along and over the top side of the flat seed, turn fruit, and skim along and over bottom side of the seed. Trim pulp remaining on the seed edges and serve with mango halves. Garnish each serving with a twist of fresh lime. Makes 2 servings.

For a refreshing dessert that requires only a minimum of preparation, serve Mangoes on the Half Shell. Accent with a lime twist.

Mango Sherbet

A tropically flavored dessert—

  1 cup water
  ½ cup sugar
  Dash salt

  • • •

  2 mangoes, peeled and sliced
  ½ cup light cream
  ¼ cup lemon juice
  2 egg whites
  ¼ cup sugar

In saucepan combine water, the ½ cup sugar, and salt; cook 5 minutes. Cool. In blender, purée mango with cream. (Or mash mango with fork and stir in cream.) Stir in cooled sugar syrup and lemon juice. Partially freeze in one 6-cup or two 3-cup refrigerator trays. Beat egg whites to soft peaks; gradually add the ¼ cup sugar, beating to stiff peaks. Turn partially frozen mixture into chilled mixer bowl; break into chunks. Beat smooth. Fold in beaten egg whites. Return to cold refrigerator tray; freeze till firm. Garnish each serving with fresh mint, if desired. Makes 6 to 8 servings.

MANHATTAN—A cocktail made with vermouth, rye or bourbon, and often a dash of bitters. (See also *Wines and Spirits*.)

MANICOTTI (*man'uh kot'ē*)—A macaroni form given the Italian name meaning "small muffs." The shape may be either plain or grooved and is often served stuffed with a flavorful filling. (See also *Macaroni*.)

Stuffed Manicotti

  1 pound ground beef
  ½ cup chopped onion
  1 large clove garlic, minced
  2 6-ounce cans tomato paste
  6 tablespoons snipped parsley
  1 tablespoon dried basil leaves,
    crushed

  • • •

  1½ pounds fresh ricotta *or* cream-style
    cottage cheese (3 cups) drained
  ⅔ cup grated romano *or* Parmesan
    cheese
  2 slightly beaten eggs
  8 manicotti shells
  ½ cup grated romano *or* Parmesan
    cheese

Brown beef lightly. Drain off fat. Add onion, garlic, tomato paste, 2 cups water, *2 tablespoons* snipped parsley, crushed basil, 1½ teaspoons salt, and dash pepper. Simmer, uncovered, about 30 minutes, stirring occasionally.

Meanwhile, combine ricotta cheese, the ⅔ cup romano cheese, eggs, remaining snipped parsley, ½ teaspoon salt, and dash pepper. Cook manicotti in boiling, salted water till just tender; drain and rinse. Use small spoon to stuff manicotti with cheese mixture.

Pour *half* the tomato-meat sauce into 11¾x 7½x1¾-inch baking dish. Arrange manicotti in row over sauce. Top with remaining sauce. Sprinkle with the ½ cup romano cheese. Bake at 350° for 30 to 35 minutes. Serves 6 to 8.

Stuffed Manicotti

Generous helpings will be demanded when→ you serve this hearty pasta stuffed with cheese and baked in a tomato-meat sauce.

MANIOC *(man'ē ok', mā' nē)*—A tropical plant that is also called cassava.

This plant's tuberous root is an important staple food in many Central and South American countries. The root is either served as a cooked vegetable similar to the potato, or used to make manioc flour. The almost tasteless manioc flour serves as a substitute for wheat flour.

In the United States, manioc is used primarily to make tapioca. The irregularly shaped tapioca particles are produced by heating manioc starch granules until they burst. (See also *Tapioca.*)

MANZANILLA OLIVE *(man' zuh nēl' yuh,-nē' uh)*—One of the large variety of Spanish olives. (See also *Olive.*)

MAPLE—A deciduous tree. Some maple varieties, particularly the sugar maple and the black maple, are valued for their sweet sap. The production of food products—syrup, sugar, and candy—from this sap is limited almost exclusively to North America.

Sometime before the arrival of colonists in North America, the Indians learned how to tap the maple tree and collect its sweet sap. These natives boiled down the sap until they got a syrupy liquid which they used as a sweetener, particularly for corn dishes. The first colonists in the area that is now the northeastern United States soon persuaded the friendly Indians to teach them the techniques involved in collecting the sap from maple trees.

By the early 1800s, the yearly sugaring time (beginning in January or February) had become firmly ingrained as a time of festivity in New England. Numerous authors of this period described the delightful aroma of bubbling maple sap, the delicious chewiness of sugar-on-snow candy, and the gala party that traditionally marked the end of the sugaring season.

However, all this fun was coupled with much hard work. Usually, the whole family helped with the cold-weather tasks of tapping the trees (boring a hole in the trunk and inserting the spout from which a bucket was hung), collecting the sap-filled buckets, transporting the sap to a sugaring camp, boiling the sap until it reached the syrup or sugar stage (it took days of

boiling and stirring to reduce 35 gallons of sap to 1 gallon of syrup), and preparing the maple sugar and syrup for storage.

Until the 1940s, the sugaring process remained essentially the same as it had been in colonial days. During the past three decades, however, the process has developed into a modern manufacturing process. Today, mechanical equipment is used for tapping the trees, fast and sanitary methods are used to transport the sap, and huge evaporator plants have replaced the multiple small sugaring houses.

Maple syrup: The sweet, viscous liquid known as maple syrup is produced by concentrating the maple sap through evaporation. Ever since the time of the American Indian, this syrup has been used primarily as a sweetener. Today, its primary use is as a topper for pancakes and waffles. Maple-blended syrups made by combining corn syrup and maple flavoring are also available at most supermarkets.

Maple sugar: If maple sap is evaporated far enough past the syrup stage, when cooled, it crystallizes into brown maple sugar. When using maple sugar as a sweetener, take into account that it is considerably sweeter than is granulated sugar.

During colonial and pioneer times, maple sugar was one of the few candies

Let breakfasters take their choice of pancake toppings by offering fluffy Maple Whip and double-flavored Maple-Apricot Syrup.

available, and even it was scarce. Although every chunk of this delicious sweet was treasured, it was even more precious when shaped in elaborate carved molds. Today, machines have replaced the carved molds, but molded maple sugar can occasionally be found at some candy counters.

Other maple products: During the boiling-down process, the consistency of maple sap goes from a liquid to a syrup to a sugar. If sap is taken off and cooled between the syrup and sugar stages, products such as maple honey and maple butter or cream are produced. The other major maple product is maple flavoring. This concentrated extract makes it easy to add the delightful maple flavor to numerous dishes.

How to use: Many people think that pancakes or waffles are incomplete without a generous amount of maple syrup poured over the stack. Remember though, the distinctive flavor of maple is also compatible with sweets such as desserts, candies, cookies, and cakes. For a delightful change from the standard vanilla or chocolate, use maple syrup or flavoring to delicately flavor chiffon pies and cakes, frostings, fudge, cookies, ice cream, and parfaits.

Although it is very impractical to boil down the maple sap to make pure maple syrup at home, you can easily make maple-flavored syrup. (See also *Flavoring.*)

Maple Skimmer

    2 teaspoons instant coffee powder
    1 14½-ounce can evaporated skim
       milk (1⅔ cups)
    ¼ cup sugar
    ½ teaspoon maple flavoring
       Coffee Ice Cubes

Combine coffee powder and 2 cups water; stir till coffee powder is dissolved. Add evaporated skim milk, sugar, and maple flavoring, stirring till sugar is dissolved. Serve over Coffee Ice Cubes. Makes 4 servings.

Coffee Ice Cubes: Using 1 teaspoon instant coffee powder for each cup water, stir together coffee powder and water. Pour into ice cube tray; freeze till solid.

The cookie jar will empty quickly when you fill it with Crisp Maple Cookies. Maple-blended syrup provides the maple flavor.

Crisp Maple Cookies

Serve these with vanilla ice cream—

    3 cups sifted all-purpose flour
    ⅓ cup sugar
    1 teaspoon salt
    1 teaspoon baking soda
    ¼ teaspoon ground nutmeg
        · · ·
    ¾ cup shortening
    1⅓ cups maple-blended syrup
    1 tablespoon vinegar
       Maple flavoring (optional)
    ½ cup finely chopped pecans

In mixing bowl sift flour, sugar, salt, baking soda, and nutmeg. Cut in shortening with pastry blender till mixture resembles coarse meal. Combine maple syrup with vinegar; add maple flavoring, if desired. Gradually stir into flour-shortening mixture. Add nuts and stir.

Drop cookie dough, about 1 tablespoon at a time, onto greased cookie sheet, *or* roll 1 tablespoon chilled dough into ball and flatten with bottom of dampened glass, on greased cookie sheet, to ⅛- to ¼-inch thickness. Bake at 400° till edges are lightly browned, about 10 to 12 minutes. Makes 4 dozen.

Maple Skimmer features two flavors—maple and coffee. For a flavor bonus, cool each serving with a coffee-flavored ice cube.

Sister Lettie's Maple-Custard Pie

1 *unbaked* 9-inch pastry shell
(See *Pastry*)
4 slightly beaten eggs
½ cup maple *or* maple-blended
syrup
½ teaspoon vanilla
¼ teaspoon salt
2½ cups milk, scalded
Few drops maple flavoring
(optional)
Ground nutmeg

Chill *unbaked* pastry shell while making filling. In mixing bowl blend eggs, maple syrup, vanilla and salt. Gradually stir in scalded milk and maple flavoring. Pour into chilled pastry shell; sprinkle with ground nutmeg. Bake at 400° till knife inserted halfway between center and outside of filling comes out clean, about 20 to 25 minutes. Cool on rack 15 to 30 minutes; then chill in refrigerator.

Maple Whip

½ cup butter or margarine
1 cup maple-blended syrup

In small mixing bowl cream butter or margarine; add maple syrup gradually. Beat till smooth and of spreading consistency. Serve whip over pancakes or waffles.

Holiday Maple Punch

1 quart coffee ice cream
8 cups milk
½ cup maple-blended syrup
Few drops maple flavoring
(optional)
. . .
Ground nutmeg

In large bowl stir ice cream to soften. Add milk, maple-blended syrup, and flavoring. Stir to blend. Top with additional spoonfuls of ice cream, if desired; sprinkle with ground nutmeg. Makes about 12 cups.

Maple Syrup

1 cup light corn syrup
½ cup brown sugar
½ cup water
. . .
Dash maple flavoring
1 tablespoon butter or margarine

In small saucepan combine light corn syrup, brown sugar, and water; cook, stirring constantly, till sugar is dissolved. Add maple flavoring and butter or margarine. Serve warm or cool. Makes about 1¾ cups.

Maple-Apricot Syrup

A delicious blend of flavors—

¾ cup maple or maple-blended syrup
¼ cup apricot preserves
1 tablespoon butter or margarine

Combine all ingredients in saucepan; heat through. Serve warm or cool. Makes 1 cup.

MARASCA CHERRY *(muh ras' kuh)*—A small cherry, primarily grown in Yugoslavia, used to make the liqueur Maraschino.

MARASCHINO CHERRY *(mar' uh skē' nō,-shē')*— A white or bleached cherry processed in a flavored sugar solution. Originally, maraschino cherries were soaked in the liqueur Maraschino, but today, a sugar syrup is used. Maraschino cherries are artificially colored either red or green.

These colorful cherries are frequently used as a garnish for cakes, fruitcakes, ice cream sundaes, banana splits, cocktails, and other beverages. They also are used to add both color and flavor to cakes, cookies, refrigerator and frozen desserts, fruit cups, fruit salads, sweet meat sauces, and candies. (See also *Cherry.*)

Cherry-Chocolate Cake

Loaded with maraschino cherries and nuts—

½ cup butter, margarine, or
    shortening
1 cup sugar
1 egg
2 1-ounce squares unsweetened
    chocolate, melted and cooled
1½ cups sifted cake flour
1 teaspoon baking soda
¾ teaspoon salt
1 cup milk
¼ cup chopped maraschino cherries
2 tablespoons maraschino cherry
    juice
½ cup chopped walnuts
    Fudge frosting

In mixing bowl stir butter, margarine, or shortening to soften. Gradually add sugar, creaming till light and fluffy. Add egg and beat well; stir in melted chocolate.

Sift together cake flour, baking soda, and salt; add to creamed mixture alternately with milk, a little at a time, beating smooth after each addition. Add chopped maraschino cherries, maraschino cherry syrup, and nuts.

Grease bottom of 8x8x2-inch square baking pan; pour in cake batter. Bake at 350° till done, about 40 minutes. Cool thoroughly. Frost top with a fudge frosting.

Maraschino Cherry Cake

½ cup shortening
2¼ cups sifted cake flour
1⅓ cups sugar
3 teaspoons baking powder
½ teaspoon salt
¼ cup maraschino cherry juice
16 maraschino cherries, chopped
½ cup milk
3 to 4 drops almond extract
4 unbeaten egg whites
½ cup chopped walnuts
1 package fluffy white frosting
    mix (for 2-layer cake)

Place shortening in mixing bowl. Sift in cake flour, sugar, baking powder, and salt. Add maraschino cherry juice, maraschino cherries, milk, and almond extract; mix till all flour is moistened. Beat vigorously 2 minutes.

Add unbeaten egg whites; beat vigorously 2 minutes longer. Fold in chopped walnuts. Bake in 2 greased and lightly floured 8x1½-inch round baking pans at 350° till cake tests done, about 30 to 35 minutes. Cool 10 minutes before removing from pans. Cool thoroughly. Fill and frost with fluffy white frosting prepared according to package directions.

Heavenly Hawaiian Cream

A deliciously rich dessert—

1 20-ounce can pineapple tidbits
¼ pound marshmallows (16), cut
    in eighths *or* 2 cups miniature
    marshmallows
¼ cup maraschino cherries, well
    drained and cut in fourths
1 cup whipping cream
¼ cup slivered blanched almonds,
    toasted
    Shredded coconut

Drain pineapple tidbits, reserving ¼ cup syrup. In mixing bowl combine drained pineapple, marshmallows, maraschino cherries, and reserved syrup. Let stand for 1 hour.

Whip cream; fold into marshmallow-fruit mixture. Spoon into dessert dishes; chill. To serve, sprinkle with toasted almonds and top with shredded coconut. Makes 6 to 8 servings.

Cherry Ice Cream

With pieces of maraschino cherry—

> ¾ cup sugar
> ½ envelope unflavored gelatin
>   (*1½ teaspoons*)
> 4 cups light cream
> 1 slightly beaten egg
> 1 teaspoon vanilla
>   Dash salt
>   . . .
> ⅓ cup maraschino cherries,
>   chopped
> 1 tablespoon maraschino cherry
>   juice

In saucepan combine sugar and unflavored gelatin. Add *half* the light cream. Cook over low heat, stirring constantly, till gelatin dissolves. Slowly stir a small amount of hot mixture into egg; mix well. Return to remaining hot mixture; cook, stirring constantly, till mixture thickens slightly, about 1 minute. Chill. Add remaining light cream, vanilla, salt, maraschino cherries, and cherry syrup.

Freeze in ice cream freezer according to manufacturer's directions. Let ripen about 4 hours. Makes about 2 quarts ice cream.

Date-Pecan Molds

> 1 8-ounce package cream cheese,
>   softened
> ¼ cup orange juice
> 1 8¾-ounce can crushed
>   pineapple, drained
> ½ cup snipped pitted dates
> ½ cup chopped pecans
> ¼ cup chopped maraschino cherries
> ½ teaspoon grated orange peel
> 1 cup whipping cream
> 8 orange slices (cut crosswise)

In mixing bowl beat together cream cheese and orange juice till fluffy. Stir in drained pineapple, dates, nuts, cherries, and orange peel. Whip cream; fold into fruit mixture.

Spoon into eight ½-cup molds *or* one 8½x 4½x2½-inch loaf dish. Freeze till firm. Let stand at room temperature 10 to 15 minutes before serving. Unmold each serving on an orange slice. Makes 8 servings.

Peach-Pineapple Ring

> 3 3-ounce packages lemon-flavored
>   gelatin
> 2 cups boiling water
> 1 29-ounce can peach halves
> 1 30-ounce can pineapple slices
> ½ cup drained maraschino
>   cherries (20)

Dissolve lemon-flavored gelatin in boiling water. Drain peaches and pineapple, reserving syrup. Combine syrups and add enough cold water to make 3 cups liquid. Add syrup mixture to dissolved gelatin. Chill till the mixture is partially set.

Alternate peach halves, cut side up, and a few of the maraschino cherries in bottom of 12½-cup ring mold. Gently pour *2 cups* partially set gelatin mixture over; chill till *almost* firm. Keep remaining gelatin at room temperature. Halve pineapple slices; place, cut edge down, around outside and inside of mold to make "scalloped" design. Center remaining maraschino cherries in half rings. Carefully pour remaining gelatin over. Chill till firm. Makes 12 to 16 servings.

This high, light Marble Chiffon Cake lives up to its name with marblelike streaks of chocolate throughout the yellow cake.

MARBLE CAKE—A varicolored cake made of two batters of contrasting color and flavor. This cake gets its name because its streaked appearance resembles the stone, marble. This marbled appearance is achieved by alternating light and dark batters in the pan, then gently swirling a spatula through the batters before baking the cake. (See also *Cake*.)

Marble Chiffon Cake

Combines chocolate and vanilla batters—

2¼ cups sifted cake flour
1½ cups sugar
  3 teaspoons baking powder
  1 teaspoon salt
½ cup salad oil
  7 egg yolks
¾ cup cold water
  1 teaspoon vanilla
  7 egg whites
½ teaspoon cream of tartar
¼ cup boiling water
  2 tablespoons sugar
  2 1-ounce squares unsweetened
      chocolate, melted and cooled
    Canned chocolate frosting
      (optional)

In a mixing bowl sift together cake flour, sugar, baking powder, and salt. Make a well in the center of the dry ingredients and add in order: salad oil, egg yolks, cold water, and vanilla. Beat till mixture is satin smooth. In a large bowl beat the egg whites with cream of tartar till *very stiff peaks* form.

Pour egg yolk mixture in thin stream over entire surface of egg whites, gently folding to blend. Remove a third of batter to separate bowl. In small mixing bowl blend together boiling water, sugar, and melted chocolate; cool. Gently fold chocolate mixture into the third portion of batter. Spoon *half* the light batter into *ungreased* 10-inch tube pan; top with *half* the chocolate batter. Repeat layers. With narrow spatula, swirl gently through batters to marble. Leave definite areas of light and dark batters.

Bake at 325° till cake tests done, about 55 minutes. Invert cake in pan; cool thoroughly. Frost with chocolate frosting, if desired.

Use a narrow metal spatula to marbleize the two batters. Don't swirl too vigorously or you'll lose the marble effect.

Daisy Marble Cake

Sift together 1 cup sifted cake flour and ½ cup sugar. Beat 1⅓ cups egg whites (10) with 1¼ teaspoons cream of tartar and ¼ teaspoon salt till soft peaks form. Gradually add 1 cup sugar, beating till stiff peaks form. Sift about ¼ of flour mixture over egg whites; fold in lightly. Repeat, folding in remaining flour mixture by thirds.

Divide batter into 2 parts. Add 1½ teaspoons finely shredded orange peel and 4 drops yellow food coloring into 4 well-beaten egg yolks; beat till very thick and lemon-colored. Fold egg yolk mixture and 2 tablespoons sifted cake flour into *half* of the batter. Fold ½ teaspoon vanilla into remaining batter.

Spoon batters alternately into *ungreased* 10-inch tube pan. Bake at 375° till cake tests done, about 35 minutes. Invert cake in pan; cool thoroughly. Frost with desired frosting.

MARBLING—The fat streaked through meat. A large amount of marbling is one of the criteria desirable in high grades of meat.

MARC *(mark)*—1. Residue left after juice is pressed from fruits, particularly grapes. 2. A spirit distilled from this residue.

MARGARINE—A table spread of butterlike consistency and flavor made of oil and skim milk or water. The oil used is most often vegetable, but a mixture of animal and vegetable oils is sometimes used. Margarine must contain 80 percent fat.

This spread was first made by a French chemist in response to a request by Napoleon III to discover a substitute for butter.

During the 1870s, margarine was introduced in the United States. Within a short time, dairymen sought legislation restricting margarine's sale in an effort to slow the progress of margarine's inroads into the butter market. In 1886, they succeeded in getting such a law passed. Among other things, this law eventually included a high tax on margarine artificially colored yellow. It wasn't until 1950 that federal taxes on margarine were dropped. Since then, most similar state laws have disappeared.

Although margarine is primarily made up of fat, it is always fortified with vitamin A and often with vitamin D. Margarine yields 36 calories per teaspoon.

In recent years, the controversy over cholesterol has involved margarine because vegetable oil margarines are lower in cholesterol than is butter.

Today, margarine is sold in two forms—solid sticks and whipped. Each solid margarine stick is ¼ pound (½ cup). Whipped margarine has the advantage of being spreadable even when very cold. Since the air beaten into this margarine increases its volume, whipped margarine must be used by weight rather than measurement.

To store margarine, cover it and keep it in the refrigerator for a few weeks or in the freezer for longer periods of time.

MARGARITA—A cocktail made of tequila, lemon or lime, and orange-flavored liqueur and served in a glass rimmed with salt.

Margarita

Moisten rim of cocktail glass with a slice of lemon or lime. Dip rim into salt. Shake together 1 jigger Tequila, 1½ tablespoons sugar *or* ½ ounce Triple Sec, 1 ounce fresh lemon or lime juice, and 3 to 4 ice cubes. Strain into glass. Garnish with lemon or lime slice.

MARGUERITE *(mar′ guh rēt′)*—A cookie made by topping a bar cookie or cracker with frosting, coconut, and nuts, then browning in the oven or under the broiler.

Marguerites

Cook 1 cup sugar, 6 tablespoons water, 1½ teaspoons light corn syrup *or* ⅛ teaspoon cream of tartar, and dash salt over low heat, stirring till sugar dissolves. Cover pan 2 to 3 minutes to dissolve sugar crystals on sides of pan. Uncover; cook to soft-ball stage (240°).

Add 6 marshmallows, quartered. Gradually add hot syrup to 1 stiffly beaten egg white, beating constantly with electric mixer. Add ½ teaspoon vanilla; beat till of spreading consistency, about 6 minutes.

Fold in ½ cup flaked coconut and 1 cup broken walnuts. Spoon onto 24 salted crackers and bake at 350° till delicately browned, about 15 minutes. Makes 2 dozen.

MARINADE *(mar′ uh nād′)*—A liquid mixture seasoned with spices and/or herbs in which food is steeped to enrich its flavor. Since the flavor of marinade often penetrates slowly, often the food is left in the marinade for several hours.

Besides providing flavor, some meat marinades have a secondary effect—they also tenderize the meat. Thus, less tender meat cuts, such as flank steak, are frequently marinated before cooking.

Armenian Marinade

Combine ½ cup *each* salad oil and chopped onion; ¼ cup *each* snipped parsley and lemon juice; 1 teaspoon *each* dried marjoram leaves, crushed, dried thyme leaves, crushed, and salt; ½ teaspoon pepper; and 1 clove garlic, minced. Use for marinade and basting. Makes 1 cup.

Easy way to marinate

Simplify clean-up by using a plastic bag in-→ stead of a bowl to hold the pork roast and marinade for Marinated Pork Roast.

Marinated Pork Roast

½ cup soy sauce
½ cup dry sherry
2 cloves garlic, minced
1 tablespoon dry mustard
1 teaspoon ground ginger
1 teaspoon dried thyme leaves,
    crushed
1 4- to 5-pound pork loin roast,
    boned, rolled, and tied
Currant Sauce

Blend first 6 ingredients. Place roast in clear plastic bag; set in deep bowl. Pour marinade in bag and close. Marinate 2 to 3 hours at room temperature or overnight in refrigerator. Occasionally press bag against meat to distribute marinade. Remove meat from marinade; place on rack in shallow roasting pan. Roast, uncovered, at 325° till meat thermometer registers 170°, about 2½ to 3 hours. Baste with marinade during last hour of cooking. Serve with Currant Sauce. Makes 10 to 12 servings.

Currant Sauce: Heat one 10-ounce jar currant jelly till melted; add 2 tablespoons dry sherry and 1 tablespoon soy sauce. Simmer 2 minutes.

Marinating meat increases its tenderness and gives it a delectable flavor. When marinating in a bowl, turn meat occasionally.

Orange-Glazed Grilled Chuck

1 12-ounce can pineapple juice
1 4/5-ounce envelope instant
    meat marinade
1 teaspoon ground ginger
¼ teaspoon ground cloves
1 3- to 4-pound beef arm roast
½ cup orange marmalade
¼ cup salad oil

Combine *1 cup* pineapple juice, instant marinade, ginger, cloves, ¼ teaspoon salt, and dash pepper. Pour over meat in shallow dish. Marinate 15 minutes, piercing meat with fork; turn several times. Remove; place meat on grill. Stir remaining pineapple juice, marmalade, and oil into marinade. Cook meat over *medium* coals for 45 minutes to 1 hour; turn and baste with marinade several times. Serves 6 to 8.

Barbecued Chuck Roast

1 3-pound chuck roast, 1½ to 2
    inches thick
⅓ cup wine vinegar
¼ cup catsup
2 tablespoons salad oil
2 tablespoons soy sauce
1 tablespoon Worcestershire sauce
1 teaspoon prepared mustard
¼ teaspoon garlic powder

Place roast in shallow dish. Combine remaining ingredients, 1 teaspoon salt, and ¼ teaspoon pepper. Pour barbecue mixture over roast and marinate 2 to 3 hours, turning twice. Place meat on grill about 6 inches from heat. Turn and baste with marinade every 10 to 15 minutes. Grill over *medium* coals about 35 to 45 minutes for medium-rare roast. Serves 6 to 8.

Marinated Three-Bean Salad

Drain one 16-ounce can cut green beans, one 16-ounce can cut wax beans, and one 15-ounce can dark red kidney beans. Combine beans and ½ cup chopped green pepper. Mix together ½ cup sugar, ⅔ cup vinegar, and ⅓ cup salad oil; pour over vegetables. Add 1 teaspoon salt and ¼ teaspoon pepper; toss. Chill overnight. Before serving, toss; drain. Serves 6 to 8.

MARINATE *(mar' uh nāt)*—To allow a food to stand in a seasoned liquid.

MARJORAM *(mär' juhr uhm)*—An herb belonging to the mint family. Other names for this herb are sweet or knotted marjoram. Although typically a perennial plant, marjoram is sown annually in colder areas because of its susceptibility to frost. Today, the flowers of this herb are incorporated in potpourris or sachets because of their delightful fragrance. Marjoram also has a wide variety of cooking uses.

Because of its spicy aroma, marjoram was used in ancient times not only as a seasoning but also as an air sweetener and in perfumes. It was even considered by some people to be a symbol of happiness; or as a charm against witchcraft.

Marjoram was originally grown in the Mediterranean area, but now it is widely cultivated. Although some marjoram is grown in the United States, most of it used in this country is imported from France, Portugal, Greece, and Romania.

There are three main varieties of this plant: sweet, pot, and wild marjoram. Each of these varieties has distinguishing characteristics and uses.

Sweet marjoram, the type commonly sold as dried, whole or ground in the supermarkets, is a low, bushy plant that grows from 12 to 18 inches high and has gray green leaves and small cream-colored flowers. This variety has a pleasing, spicy, sweet flavor that combines well with other herbs. It is often found in fine herb mixtures and is also one of the ingredients used in poultry seasoning mixtures.

Pot marjoram, primarily an ornamental plant, can be grown indoors. However, it is seldom used for its herb flavor.

Wild marjoram, by far the hardiest of the three varieties, has a very strong flavor. It is a tall plant and is commonly known as the herb oregano. Due to the flavor differences, wild and sweet marjoram are seldom interchanged in recipes.

You will find a touch of fresh or dried marjoram delightful in soups or stews, in seafood and poultry dishes, with roasts, eggs, vegetables, salads, and sauces. Remember to use the herb with discretion for it is highly aromatic. (See also *Herb.*)

Fruited Chicken Salad

3 cups cubed cooked chicken
1 cup diced celery
1 11-ounce can mandarin oranges, drained
1 8¾-ounce can pineapple tidbits, drained
½ cup toasted slivered almonds
¾ cup mayonnaise or salad dressing
½ teaspoon salt
⅛ teaspoon ground marjoram

Combine first 5 ingredients. Chill thoroughly. Blend together mayonnaise, salt, and marjoram. Add to chicken mixture. Toss together lightly to coat all ingredients. Serves 6.

Beef and Sprouts

2 pounds beef stew meat, cut in 1½-inch cubes
2 tablespoons shortening
1 clove garlic, minced
2 medium onions, sliced
2 tablespoons vinegar
1 teaspoon paprika
1 teaspoon salt
¼ teaspoon dried marjoram leaves, crushed
1 cup water
. . .
½ teaspoon grated lemon peel
½ teaspoon caraway seed
1 10-ounce package frozen Brussels sprouts
. . .
2 tablespoons all-purpose flour
¼ cup cold water
Hot cooked noodles

In large saucepan brown meat in hot shortening; remove meat. Add garlic and onions; cook till tender. Stir in vinegar, paprika, salt, and marjoram. Add meat and the 1 cup water; cover and simmer 1 hour and 20 minutes. Add lemon peel, caraway seed, and frozen Brussels sprouts. Cover; bring to boiling over high heat. Reduce heat and simmer till sprouts are tender, about 10 minutes. Blend together flour and the ¼ cup cold water; stir into stew. Cook and stir till thickened and bubbly. Serve over cooked noodles. Makes 6 servings.

MARMALADE—A jellylike product containing pieces of fruit and fruit peel. Although other fruits and berries may be used, citrus fruits, especially oranges, are usually used for marmalade. (See also *Jelly*.)

Marmalade Pan Bread

A delicious use for marmalade and bran cereal—

In mixing bowl combine 1 cup whole bran cereal and ¾ cup milk. Let stand 1 to 2 minutes. Add 1 egg and ¼ cup shortening; beat well. Sift together 1 cup sifted all-purpose flour, ¼ cup sugar, 2½ teaspoons baking powder, and ½ teaspoon salt. Add dry ingredients to cereal mixture, stirring just till combined. Spread batter in greased 9x9x2-inch baking pan. Spoon on ½ cup orange marmalade; press marmalade lightly into batter. Bake at 400° for 25 minutes. Cut in squares. Serve warm.

Hot, buttered toast generously spread with homemade Blueberry Marmalade is a special treat for breakfast or an evening snack.

Orange Marmalade

    4 medium oranges
    1 medium lemon
1½ cups water
 ¼ teaspoon baking soda
        · · ·
    6 cups sugar
 ½ 6-ounce bottle liquid fruit
       pectin

Remove peels from oranges and lemon. Scrape excess white from peel; cut peels in *very fine* shreds. Add water and baking soda. Bring to boiling; simmer, covered, for 10 minutes.

Remove white membrane from peeled fruit; section fruit (discard seeds), working over bowl to catch juice. Combine pulp, reserved juice, and cooked peel. Cook slowly 20 minutes.

Measure 3 cups fruit-peel mixture; add sugar. Bring to boiling; cook 5 minutes. Remove from heat; immediately stir in liquid fruit pectin. Skim and stir 5 minutes. Ladle into hot, scalded glasses; seal. Makes six ½-pint glasses.

Marmalade-Ham Squares

Topped with a tangy glaze—

1½ cups packaged herb-seasoned
       stuffing mix
    2 cups milk
1½ pounds ground fresh pork
1½ pounds ground fully cooked ham
 ½ cup chopped onion
 ¼ teaspoon salt
        · · ·
    1 cup orange marmalade
    2 tablespoons vinegar
    1 teaspoon dry mustard
 ¼ teaspoon ground cinnamon
 ¼ teaspoon ground cloves
    Orange sections

Soak stuffing mix in milk for 5 minutes. Add ground meats, onion, and salt; mix well. Lightly pack into 9x9x2-inch baking dish. Bake at 350° for 1¼ hours. Spoon off drippings.

For glaze, mix orange marmalade, vinegar, dry mustard, cinnamon, and cloves; spread over loaf. Bake 10 minutes longer. Allow to stand a few minutes before cutting in squares. Trim with orange sections. Makes 9 to 12 servings.

Marmalade-Plum Pie

1½ pounds fresh Italian plums
⅓ cup sugar
¾ cup water
2 tablespoons cornstarch
¼ teaspoon salt
2 tablespoons butter or margarine

. . .

Pastry for 2-crust 9-inch pie
   (See *Pastry*)
⅓ cup orange marmalade

Pit and quarter plums (about 3 cups). Combine plums and water. Bring to boiling and cook 3 to 4 minutes. Combine sugar, cornstarch, and salt; stir into plum mixture. Cook the mixture slowly, stirring constantly till it is thickened and bubbly; remove from heat. Stir in butter or margarine; cool.

Line 9-inch pie plate with pastry; spread bottom with orange marmalade. Fill with cooled plum mixture. Adjust top crust, cutting slits for escape of steam. Seal and flute edge. Bake at 425° for 30 to 35 minutes.

Blueberry Marmalade

Delicious on hot, buttered English muffins—

1 medium orange
1 medium lemon
¾ cup water
3 cups crushed blueberries

. . .

5 cups sugar
½ 6-ounce bottle liquid fruit
   pectin

Remove peels from orange and lemon. Scrape excess white from peel; cut peel in *very fine* shreds. Place in very large saucepan. Add water. Bring to boiling; simmer, covered, for 10 minutes, stirring occasionally.

Remove white membrane from peeled fruit; finely chop pulp (discard seeds). Add to peel with crushed blueberries. Cover; simmer 12 minutes. Add sugar. Bring to *full rolling boil; boil hard 1 minute*, stirring constantly. Remove from heat; immediately stir in liquid fruit pectin. Skim off foam; stir and skim for 7 minutes. Ladle into hot scalded jars. Seal at once. Makes six ½-pint jars.

Marmalade-Fig Bars

Accompany these delicious, layered bar cookies with a cup of steaming hot coffee or tea—

1½ cups sifted all-purpose flour
1 teaspoon baking powder
½ teaspoon salt
1½ cups quick-cooking rolled oats
1 cup brown sugar
¾ cup butter or margarine
1 cup chopped dried figs
1 cup orange marmalade

In mixing bowl sift together all-purpose flour, baking powder, and salt. Add quick-cooking rolled oats and brown sugar. With pastry blender, cut in butter or margarine till mixture is crumbly. Stir in chopped figs.

Pat ⅔ of fig-rolled oats mixture into 13x9x2-inch baking pan. Spread with orange marmalade. Sprinkle remaining fig-rolled oats mixture over top. Bake at 375° for 30 to 35 minutes. Cool; cut into bars. Makes about 2 dozen.

MARMITE (*mär′mĭt, mär mēt′*)—A deep soup kettle usually made of earthenware.

MAROR (*mä rôr′*)—Any of several bitter-tasting herbs eaten by the Jews during the celebration of Passover. Maror is served as a reminder of the bitter hardships endured by the Jews during the years they were enslaved in Egypt.

MARRON (*mar′ uhn, muh rōn′*)—The French word for chestnut. Imported canned marrons are available in the United States in several forms, including puréed, chopped, and whole packed in water, plus whole or chopped marrons in syrup.

MARRON GLACÉ—Chestnut glazed with a vanilla-flavored syrup. This delicious confection may be eaten as a candy or used in desserts or as a garnish.

MARROW—1. The soft tissue found in the center cavity of animal bones. Marrow, especially beef marrow, is prized as a delicacy. It is used cooked as an appetizer spread as well as in soups, stews, and sauces. 2. British name for summer squash.

MARSHMALLOW—A soft candy made of sugar, corn syrup, egg white and/or gelatin, and flavoring. Marshmallows once were made from a jellylike gum extracted from the roots of the marshmallow plant. However, to save time and money, gelatin or other gums now are used.

Marshmallows range from very soft to very firm varieties and include items such as circus peanuts, marshmallow eggs, colored marshmallows, and the popular, soft, puffy, white marshmallow. This sugar-dusted confection is delicious eaten as a candy or toasted over an open fire till golden brown outside and slightly melted inside.

As an ingredient, marshmallows have numerous uses. They add flavor and creaminess to gelatin salads, candy, puddings, and other desserts. Marshmallows make a quick cake frosting or sweet potato topping when melted slightly under the broiler. Miniature marshmallows or large marshmallows cut up can be used to decorate cakes or as a garnish for dishes such as meats and salads. For a special dessert, add a few marshmallows to chocolate pudding. Combine fruits and marshmallows with a sour cream dressing for a refreshing salad. In any event, keep this versatile confection on hand. (See also *Candy*.)

Chocolate Dessert Duet

    ¼ cup semisweet chocolate pieces
  2⅔ cups miniature marshmallows
    1 egg
    ¼ teaspoon vanilla
    ½ cup whipping cream
    2 tablespoons slivered almonds,
      toasted

Combine chocolate pieces, marshmallows, 2 tablespoons water, and dash salt in top of double boiler. Cook and stir over hot water till completely melted. Separate egg. Beat egg yolk slightly. Stir in small amount of chocolate mixture; return to hot mixture. Cook, stirring constantly, for 2 minutes. Remove from heat; add vanilla. Beat till smooth; cool.

Beat egg white till stiff peaks form. Fold into chocolate mixture. Whip cream; fold into chocolate mixture. Spoon into sherbets. Top with almonds. Chill. Makes 4 servings.

Enticing Chocolate-Marshmallow Parfaits are easy to prepare. Simply layer vanilla ice cream with the creamy sauce made with chocolate pieces and marshmallow creme.

Marshmallows

2 envelopes unflavored gelatin
    (2 tablespoons)
1 cup granulated sugar
1 cup light corn syrup
1 egg white
  Confectioners' sugar

Soften gelatin in ½ cup cold water. In saucepan combine granulated sugar, corn syrup, and ⅓ cup water. Cook to soft-ball stage (240°), stirring only till sugar dissolves. Remove from heat; stir in gelatin to dissolve. Let cool 10 minutes. Beat egg white to stiff peaks. Slowly add syrup, beating on high speed of electric mixer till candy stands in soft peaks.

Pour onto plain brown paper and spread in 12x10-inch rectangle. Let stand overnight. Dust with confectioners' sugar; turn over on another piece of paper. Moisten brown paper slightly to remove from candy. Cut in desired size pieces. Makes 1½ pounds.

Peach-Marshmallow Pie

1 29-ounce can peach slices
¼ cup sugar
1 envelope unflavored gelatin
    (1 tablespoon)
1 cup miniature marshmallows
1 beaten egg
1 teaspoon shredded lemon peel
4 teaspoons lemon juice
½ cup whipping cream
1 9-inch *baked* pastry shell,
    cooled (*See Pastry*)

Drain peach slices, reserving 1¼ cups syrup. Reserve 6 peach slices; cut up remainder. Combine sugar, unflavored gelatin, and ¼ teaspoon salt. Blend in reserved syrup. Add miniature marshmallows. Cook, stirring constantly, till marshmallows melt. Blend some of hot mixture into beaten egg; return to hot mixture. Cook, stirring constantly, for 2 to 3 minutes.

Add shredded lemon peel and lemon juice. Cover; cool till mixture begins to set. Whip cream. Fold cut-up peaches and whipped cream into partially set gelatin mixture. Spoon into cooled pastry shell. Chill at least 3 to 4 hours. Top with reserved peach slices and additional whipped cream, if desired.

Broiled Party Cake

The quick broiled frosting uses apricot preserves, coconut, and miniature marshmallows—

1 package 2-layer-size yellow
    cake mix
1 12-ounce jar apricot preserves
    (1 cup)
1 tablespoon lemon juice
1 3½-ounce can flaked coconut
    (1⅓ cups)
1½ cups miniature marshmallows

Prepare cake mix using package directions. Bake in greased and floured 13x9x2-inch baking pan at 350° about 35 minutes. Combine apricot preserves and lemon juice; stir in coconut and miniature marshmallows. Spread atop hot cake. Broil 3 to 4 inches from heat till golden, about 1 minute. Cool.

Marshmallow Puffs

Children will love these—

4 cups puffed rice
¼ cup butter or margarine
3 cups miniature marshmallows
2 tablespoons natural-flavor
    malted milk powder
1 tablespoon instant coffee
    powder
½ cup semisweet chocolate pieces

Heat puffed rice in shallow baking pan at 350° for 10 minutes. Pour into well-greased, large bowl. In saucepan heat butter or margarine and miniature marshmallows over low heat till marshmallows are melted. Stir in natural-flavor malted milk powder and instant coffee powder. Pour over puffed rice; stir till evenly coated. Press into well-greased 13x9x2-inch baking pan. Melt semisweet chocolate pieces over low heat, stirring constantly. Drizzle chocolate over cereal mixture. Refrigerate till serving time. Cut into bars. Makes about 2 dozen.

MARSHMALLOW CREME—A thick, creamy product made of corn syrup, sugar, egg whites, and flavoring. Its appearance resembles that of melted marshmallows.

Chocolate–Marshmallow Parfaits

1 6-ounce package semisweet
    chocolate pieces (1 cup)
½ cup evaporated milk
½ 7-ounce jar marshmallow creme
    Vanilla ice cream
    Toasted coconut

In saucepan combine semisweet chocolate pieces and evaporated milk. Cook over low heat, stirring constantly, till chocolate is melted. Remove from heat; stir in marshmallow creme. Cool. Alternate layers of vanilla ice cream and chocolate sauce in parfait glasses. Top with toasted coconut. Makes 1¼ cups sauce.

MARTINI—A popular cocktail made with gin and vermouth. (See also *Cocktail*.)

Traditional Martini

1 jigger dry gin *or* vodka
½ jigger dry vermouth
    Cracked ice
    Lemon twist or olive

Combine gin or vodka, dry vermouth, and cracked ice. Stir and strain into a chilled cocktail glass. Add lemon twist or olive. Makes 1.

Dry Martini

Combine 5 parts dry gin *or* vodka, 1 part dry vermouth, and cracked ice. Stir and strain into a chilled cocktail glass. Garnish with a lemon twist or an olive. Makes 1.

Extra Dry Martini

Combine 7 parts dry gin *or* vodka (if only extra dry, not extra strong, use 80-proof), 1 part dry vermouth, and cracked ice. Stir and strain into a chilled cocktail glass. Add a lemon twist or an olive.

MARYLAND FRIED CHICKEN—A style of cooking chicken in which coated chicken pieces are browned, then simmered in milk.

Maryland Fried Chicken

1 slightly beaten egg
1¼ cups milk
⅔ cup fine cracker crumbs
½ teaspoon salt
    Dash pepper
1 2½- to 3-pound ready-to-cook
    broiler-fryer chicken,
    cut up
3 to 4 tablespoons shortening

Combine egg and ¼ *cup* of the milk. Mix cracker crumbs with salt and pepper. Dip chicken pieces into egg mixture; then roll in crumbs. In heavy skillet brown chicken in hot shortening; turn with tongs. Add remaining milk. Cover tightly and simmer 35 minutes; uncover and cook until tender, about 10 minutes. Make gravy from drippings. Makes 4 servings.

MARZIPAN (*mär' zuh pan'*)—A confection made of almond paste, sugar, and sometimes egg whites. The mixture is traditionally shaped into small fruits or leaves and then allowed to harden. Marzipan has long been a favorite Christmas candy.

Marzipan

2 cups sugar
1½ cups boiling water
⅛ teaspoon cream of tartar *or*
    2 tablespoons light corn syrup
1 8-ounce can almond paste
    Red, green, and yellow food
    coloring
    Leaves and berry hulls

Butter sides of heavy 1½-quart saucepan. In it combine sugar, water, and cream of tartar *or* corn syrup. Stir over medium heat till sugar dissolves and mixture boils. Cook without stirring to soft-ball stage (240°). Immediately pour onto platter. *Do not* scrape pan.

Cool till candy feels only slightly warm to the touch, about 30 minutes; do not move. Using spatula or wooden spoon, scrape candy from edge of platter toward center, then work till creamy and stiff. Knead till smooth and free from lumps. Wrap; place in covered container to ripen for 24 hours.

Delight both children and adults with a colorful array of apples, peaches, bananas, pears, and strawberries made from Marzipan.

Warm ripened mixture in bowl over hot water and work to a smooth cream (about 2 minutes), adding a few drops of water, if needed. Work in almond paste till smooth. Place in bowl, cover with damp cloth, and let ripen several hours. Divide in parts; tint to desired color with red, yellow, or green food coloring and shape into fruits as described below. Dry fruits overnight on their sides on waxed paper. Next day, add blushes or sugar.

Pears: Tint Marzipan yellow. Mold pear shape, using 2 teaspoons Marzipan for each. Add cloves for blossom ends and press on leaves. Next day, pat or brush with a pink blush, using red food coloring mixed with water.

Peaches: Tint Marzipan orange. Mold balls, using 1½ teaspoons each. Flatten on both ends. Crease one side with knife. Add clove at one end, leaves at the other. Next day, add pink blush, using red food coloring mixed with water.

Apples: Tint Marzipan green. Mold balls, using 1½ teaspoons each. Add clove at one end, leaves at the other end. Next day, add red blush, using red food coloring.

Bananas: Tint Marzipan yellow. Mold banana shapes, using 2 teaspoons each. Next day, tint ends green and streak with cocoa dissolved in equal amount of water.

Strawberries: Tint Marzipan red. Roll in balls, using 1 teaspoon each. Shape point at one end and flatten the other. Add hull. Let dry overnight. Brush with corn syrup; roll in red sugar. Dry thoroughly.

MASH—1. Crushed grain or malt that has been soaked in water. Mash is used in the manufacture of some kinds of liquor. 2. To press or beat a food until all lumps are removed. Cooked potatoes are commonly mashed before serving.

MATÉ *(mä′ tä, mat′ ä)*—A slightly bitter beverage that resembles tea. This beverage, popular in South American countries such as Brazil, Chili, Uruguay, and Paraguay, is also called yerba maté and Paraguay tea.

The dried leaves of a shrub that resembles holly are used to make this slightly stimulating beverage. Traditionally, maté is brewed in a hollow gourd and sipped through a *bombilla* (a tube with a strainer at the tip). In recent years, however, maté has been served in small cups.

Like tea, maté may be drunk as it is or flavored with sugar and/or the peel from citrus fruits, particularly oranges.

Mashing fruit with a slotted kitchen utensil before adding it to ice cream mix assures that the fruit will be evenly distributed.

MATZO (*mät′ suh,-sō*)—An unleavened bread made of flour and water. The significance of matzo, according to the Jewish religion, dates back to the flight of the Jews from Egypt when unleavened bread was eaten because there was no time to let the bread rise. This bread is eaten by Jews during the celebration of Passover in remembrance of the flight of their ancestors.

Today, matzoth, available plain or flavored with onion, cheese, and chocolate, are quite popular as an appetizer or snack food. (See also *Jewish Cookery*.)

MAYONNAISE—A spoonable, uncooked dressing made of eggs or egg yolks, oil, vinegar or lemon juice, and seasonings. Commercial mayonnaise contains at least 65 percent oil.

Unlike French dressing which has similar ingredients, mayonnaise contains egg yolk which acts as a stabilizing ingredient. This means that mayonnaise does not separate as readily as French dressing does.

The commercial product labeled salad dressing resembles mayonnaise, but it doesn't contain as much oil. A cooked starch paste is usually substituted for the oil.

Nutritional value: Although mayonnaise contains small amounts of some of the vitamins and minerals, it is principally fat. One tablespoon of mayonnaise contributes approximately 100 calories to the diet.

Basic preparation and storage: Even though many homemakers consider mayonnaise hard to make, it is easy to prepare delicious mayonnaise by simply following directions. Remember that the most important thing is to add the oil to the egg-liquid mixture

---

If mayonnaise fails

Occasionally mayonnaise fails to form an emulsion and you end up with a separated mixture. If this happens, restore the mayonnaise by very slowly *beating the separated mixture into an egg yolk*. This remedy will not work if you mistakenly beat the egg yolk into the separated mayonnaise mixture.

---

very slowly at first, no more than a teaspoon at a time. As the oil and liquid form an emulsion, the oil can be added slightly faster but still with restraint.

Once mayonnaise has been prepared or opened, store it in the refrigerator. Mayonnaise-containing mixtures are particularly good media for the growth of some types of food poisoning microorganisms, so be sure to keep these foods refrigerated.

Uses in cooking: Quite naturally, the primary use of mayonnaise is in salad dressings. A dollop of mayonnaise is a natural accompaniment for a lettuce wedge or a gelatin vegetable salad. When the salad contains fruit, make the dressing by mixing a little mayonnaise with whipped cream or marshmallow creme. For other simple dressings, start with mayonnaise and add shredded cheese, fruit juice, herbs, yogurt, chili sauce, or catsup.

When cold meat sandwiches are on the menu, mayonnaise is an essential ingredient. You can either spread mayonnaise on the bread before assembling the sandwich or use it in the sandwich filling.

Casseroles, gelatin salads, canapés, and many other dishes also use mayonnaise as an ingredient. (See also *Salad Dressing*.)

Mayonnaise

In mixer bowl mix 1 teaspoon salt, ½ teaspoon dry mustard, ¼ teaspoon paprika, and dash cayenne; blend in 2 egg yolks. Add 2 tablespoons vinegar; mix well. Beating with rotary or electric beater, slowly add ¼ cup salad oil (1 teaspoon at a time). Add 1¾ cups salad oil in increasing amounts, alternating last ½ cup oil with 2 tablespoons lemon juice. Beat in 1 tablespoon hot water. Makes 2 cups.

Pink Fruit Mayonnaise

⅓ cup cranberry juice cocktail
1 cup mayonnaise
2 tablespoons toasted chopped almonds

Stir cranberry juice cocktail and dash salt into mayonnaise. Chill. Add nuts. Makes 1½ cups.

Blender Mayonnaise

This mayonnaise is extra-easy—

    1 large egg
    1 tablespoon vinegar
    ½ teaspoon salt
    ¼ teaspoon dry mustard
    ⅛ teaspoon paprika
      Dash cayenne
    1 cup salad oil
    1 tablespoon lemon juice

Combine egg, vinegar, salt, dry mustard, paprika, and cayenne in blender container. Cover; blend till mixed. With blender running slowly, gradually pour half of the salad oil into blender container. (When necessary, stop blender and use rubber spatula to scrape sides down.) Add lemon juice. Slowly pour remaining salad oil into blender container with the blender running slowly. Makes about 1¼ cups.

Herb Dressing

    1 cup mayonnaise
    ⅓ cup finely chopped onion
    ½ teaspoon grated lemon peel
    2 tablespoons lemon juice
    2 cloves garlic, minced
    1 tablespoon dry sherry
    2 teaspoons Worcestershire sauce
    ½ teaspoon dried mixed salad
        herbs

Mix mayonnaise, finely chopped onion, grated lemon peel, lemon juice, minced garlic, sherry, Worcestershire sauce, and dried mixed salad herbs. Chill. Serve over lettuce. Makes 1½ cups.

Marshmallow Dressing

    1 tablespoon orange juice
    1 tablespoon lemon juice
    ½ 7-ounce jar marshmallow creme
           • • •
    ¼ cup mayonnaise

Gradually add orange and lemon juice to marshmallow creme. Beat at high speed on electric mixer till fluffy. Fold in mayonnaise. Serve over fruit or gelatin salads. Makes 1¼ cups.

Blue Cheese Dressing

    2 cups mayonnaise
    1 cup crumbled blue cheese
    ¼ cup dairy sour cream
    ¼ cup vinegar
    2 tablespoons sugar
    1 clove garlic, minced

In mixing bowl combine mayonnaise, crumbled blue cheese, sour cream, vinegar, sugar, and minced garlic. Beat till fluffy. Chill. Serve over salad greens or lettuce. Makes 3½ cups.

Yogurt Dressing

    1 cup yogurt
    2 tablespoons mayonnaise
    1 teaspoon sugar
      Dash lemon juice
      Dash salt

Combine all ingredients. Chill. Serve over fruit or gelatin salads. Makes about 1 cup.

Poppy Seed Dressing

    ½ cup mayonnaise
    2 tablespoons sugar
    1 tablespoon poppy seed
    1 tablespoon lemon juice

Combine all ingredients. Chill. Serve over fruit or gelatin salads. Makes about ¾ cup.

Creamy Mayonnaise

    ½ cup whipping cream
    1 cup mayonnaise

Whip whipping cream; fold into mayonnaise. Chill. Serve on fruit salads. Makes about 2 cups.

Chili Mayonnaise

    ½ cup chili sauce
    1 cup mayonnaise

Stir chili sauce into mayonnaise. Chill. Serve over lettuce or tossed salads. Makes 1½ cups.

Zippy Beet Dressing

1 8-ounce can diced beets
½ cup mayonnaise
1½ teaspoons prepared horseradish
Dash salt

. . .

1 medium head lettuce

Thoroughly drain diced beets, reserving liquid. Mash beets slightly with fork; stir in mayonnaise, horseradish, and dash salt. Add beet juice if needed to make mixture of desired consistency. Chill, if desired. Core lettuce and cut it into 6 wedges. Spoon on beet dressing. Makes about 6 servings.

Beef Salad Sandwiches

Mix 1½ cups ground cooked roast beef; ⅓ cup mayonnaise; 1 tablespoon pickle relish, drained; 1 tablespoon finely chopped onion; 1 teaspoon prepared mustard; and ¼ teaspoon salt. Spread 8 slices bread with softened butter or margarine. Spread meat mixture on *four* slices. Top with lettuce, then remaining bread. Serves 4.

Chef's Rice Salad

1½ cups water
½ teaspoon salt
1 10-ounce package frozen peas
1 cup packaged precooked rice
¾ cup mayonnaise
¼ cup chopped dill pickle
1 teaspoon grated onion
Dash pepper

. . .

Lettuce
½ 12-ounce can chopped ham, cut in thin strips (1 cup)
2 ounces Swiss cheese, cut in thin strips (½ cup)

Bring water and salt to boiling. Add frozen peas to water; return to boiling and boil 2 minutes. Stir in uncooked packaged precooked rice; cover. Remove from heat; let stand 5 minutes. Stir in mayonnaise, dill pickle, grated onion, and pepper; chill thoroughly. Serve on lettuce; top the salad with ham and Swiss cheese strips. Makes about 4 or 5 servings.

Macaroni-Cheese Cups

½ 7-ounce package uncooked elbow macaroni (1 cup)
8 medium green peppers
2 cups cubed fully cooked ham
4 ounces sharp process American cheese, diced (1 cup)
¼ cup diced sweet pickle
2 tablespoons chopped canned pimiento
2 tablespoons finely chopped onion
½ cup mayonnaise
2 teaspoons prepared mustard

Cook macaroni following package directions; drain and cool. Cut off pepper tops; remove seeds and membrane. Cook peppers in boiling, salted water for 5 minutes; plunge immediately into cold water. Combine cooked macaroni, ham, cheese, pickle, pimiento, and onion.

Blend together mayonnaise, mustard, and ¼ teaspoon salt; toss lightly with macaroni mixture. Season inside of peppers with salt; fill with macaroni mixture. Chill thoroughly. Serve on lettuce-lined plates. Makes 8 servings.

Cherry Salad Supreme

1 3-ounce package raspberry-flavored gelatin
1 21-ounce can cherry pie filling
1 3-ounce package lemon-flavored gelatin
1 3-ounce package cream cheese, softened
⅓ cup mayonnaise
1 8¾-ounce can crushed pineapple
½ cup whipping cream
1 cup miniature marshmallows
2 tablespoons chopped nuts

Dissolve raspberry gelatin in 1 cup boiling water; stir in cherry pie filling. Turn into 9x9x2-inch baking dish; chill till partially set. Dissolve lemon gelatin in 1 cup boiling water. Beat together cream cheese and mayonnaise. Gradually add lemon gelatin. Stir in *undrained* pineapple. Whip cream; fold into lemon gelatin mixture with miniature marshmallows. Spread atop cherry layer; top with chopped nuts. Chill till firm. Makes 12 servings.

MAY WINE—A punch made of wine flavored with the herb woodruff. This beverage is particularly popular in Germany during the month of May. It is usually garnished with fresh fruit, such as oranges, apples, lemons, strawberries, and pineapples.

McINTOSH APPLE—A juicy, all-purpose, winter apple characterized by a red and green skin and an oval shape. The spicy, yet pleasantly tart flavor of this particular variety makes McIntosh apples suitable for eating either raw or cooked. Although many are shipped to other areas, most of the McIntosh apples in the United States are grown in the eastern part of the country. McIntosh apples are available from September through May. (See also *Apple*.)

MEAD—A fermented beverage in which the principal ingredients are water and honey.

The early Teutons, who occupied what is now Germany, were particularly fond of this drink. It is not known when mead was first made in England, but early English writings mention it as the drink of kings. At one time it was the most popular alcoholic beverage in England.

During the Middle Ages, the popularity of mead spread throughout Europe. This mead resembled sparkling wine.

Gradually, other alcoholic beverages took the place of mead, and today, the production of mead is almost a forgotten art.

MEAL—1. A coarsely ground cereal grain. In this sense, meal is usually used with the name of the grain such as cornmeal. 2. The food eaten at one time. This could mean that every time you eat anything, you are eating a meal, but the term is usually restricted to those few times a day when several dishes at a time are served.

In the United States, 3 meals a day—breakfast, lunch or dinner, and dinner or supper—are customary. However, many people adjust their meal pattern to suit their life style and individual situation.

Although the primary purpose of meals is to satisfy the nutritional needs of the body, mealtime has also become a special time of conversation and companionship in many families. A pleasant, unhurried meal also affords the diner time to relax.

MEAL PLANNING—The process of preparing menus for the family's meals. Although the technique may vary from planning on paper several days in advance to mental planning on the day of the meal, the objectives of meal planning should be to serve meals that are nutritious, attractive, and delicious. The homemaker must combine science and skill to achieve this.

The scientific part of meal planning involves knowing the nutritional needs of your family and planning menus which fulfill these needs. The easiest way to plan nutritional meals is to follow the Basic Four Food Groups — Milk Group, Meat Group, Vegetable-Fruit Group, and Bread-Cereal Group. For a well-balanced daily diet, each family member should eat at least two servings from the Milk Group (children 9 to 12 need three servings and teen-agers need four or more servings), at least two servings from the Meat Group, four servings from the Vegetable-Fruit Group, and four servings from the Bread-Cereal Group. (See also *Nutrition*.)

The following meal planning steps will help you incorporate foods from the Basic Four into the daily menus you plan.

1. Select a main dish that will provide each family member with at least one serving from the Meat Group.

2. Add a complementary food from the Bread-Cereal Group.

3. Include a hot or cold vegetable dish. A good vegetable source of vitamin A should be served at least every other day.

4. Choose a fruit or vegetable salad that complements the main dish.

5. Top off the meal with a dessert. If your family balks at drinking milk, help fulfill their daily requirement by using milk frequently in desserts.

6. Select a hot or cold beverage. This is another excellent place to fulfill the daily milk requirement.

In the common pattern of three meals a day—breakfast, lunch or dinner, and dinner or supper—each meal does not need to follow all of the above steps. However, remember to make sure that the day's menu as a whole fulfills the daily requirements.

Satisfying the body's nutritional needs is the primary purpose for eating. However, in the affluent societies of today, food

Meal Planning Chart		
Main Dish	Starchy Complement	Vegetable
Beef Pot Roast*	Pot Roasted Potatoes Baked Potato	Pot Roasted Carrots & Onions Italian Eggplant*
Deviled Swiss Steak*	Scalloped Potatoes* Mashed Potatoes	Buttered Green Beans Diced Beets
Lasagne*	Buttered French Bread Butterhorns*	Italian Green Beans Relishes
Veal Chops*	Noodles Romano* Oven-Browned Potatoes	Buttered Green Beans with Almonds Sauerkraut
Fruit Stuffed Pork*	Baked Potatoes Baked Sweet Potatoes*	Buttered Brussels Sprouts Corn on the Cob
Oven Barbecued Ribs*	Buttered French Bread Mashed Potatoes	Asparagus Casserole* Sauerkraut
Ham Loaf*	Scalloped Potato Bake* Candied Sweets*	Broccoli Spears Buttered Green Peas
Roast Leg of Lamb*	Baked Potato Butter-Baked Rice*	Zucchini Parmesan* Creamed Peas
French Fried Liver*	Hash-Browns*	Baked Squash Scalloped Corn Supreme*
Perfect Fried Chicken*	French Fries* Mashed Potatoes	Carrots Brussels Sprouts Polonaise*
Turkey-Noodle Bake*	Sourdough Bread*	Green Peas Harvard Beets*
Broiled Cornish Game Hen*	Wild Rice and Mushrooms* Sweet Potatoes Royale*	Buttered Broccoli Spears Cut Green Beans
Fried Fish*	Cottage Fried Potatoes* French Bread	Artichoke Velvet* Corn on the Cob
Lobster*	Poppy Seed Rolls Bread Sticks	Celery Oriental* Asparagus
*All starred recipes appear in these encyclopedias. See index for pages.		

Meal Planning Chart		
Salad	Dessert	Accent
Waldorf Salad* Lettuce Wedge with Italian Salad Dressing	Pineapple Chiffon Cake* Sherbet	Pickles Sour Cream Potato Topper
Spicy Apricot Mold* Frozen Fruit Slices*	Chocolate Cake Coffee and Sandies*	Almonds (on beans) Oysters on Half Shell (appetizer)
Original Caesar Salad* Tossed Green Salad	Hot Fruit Compote* Peach Pie*	Frosted Cocktail* (appetizer)
Sliced Tomatoes Cheese Stuffed Celery Sticks	Apple Pie Two-Berry Parfaits*	Cheddar Cheese Wedge (on pie) Vanilla Wafer (with dessert)
Italian Salad Bowl* Wilted Lettuce Toss*	Kona Coffee Torte* Raspberry Sherbet	Pineapple Juice (appetizer) Brown-Eyed Susan Cookies*
Citrus Salad Tossed Vegetable Salad	Banana-Apricot Pie* Strawberry Floating Island*	Small Mints (after dinner)

Green Goddess Salad*
 	
Pineapple Rings with
  Stewed Prune Centers
	Swedish Fruit Soup*
	
	Butterscotch Sundae
	  (Butterscotch Sauce*)
		Pimiento Strips
		  (for broccoli spears)
		Horseradish Sauce* (for ham)

Jubilee Salad Mold* Fresh Fruit Salad	Citrus Chiffon Pie* Regal Plum Pudding*	Mint Sauce* Honey-Lime Dressing*

Fresh Fruit Toss
 	
Cucumber Ring Supreme*
	Ice Cream with
	  Chocolate Wafer
	Fresh Fruit Plate
		Melted Marshmallows
		  (atop squash)
		Vanilla Wafer

Marinated Three-Bean Salad* Orange Gelatin Salad	Stirred Custard with Raspberries Parfait and Cookie	 Perfect Gravy*
Sunshine Salad* Fresh Fruit Salad	Chocolate Fudge Cake* Ice Cream	Gazpacho* (appetizer) Honey-Lime Dressing* (for salad)
Pink Pear Salad* Lettuce Slice with Dressing	Assorted Cookies Baked Alaska*	Demitasse* Russian Dressing* (for salad)
Pineapple and Melon Balls Calico Vegetable Bowl*	Pumpkin Pie* Baked Apple*	Whipped Cream Dollop (for pie) Hard Sauce* (for apple)

Tossed Green Salad
Wilted Spinach Salad*
	Raspberry Bombe*
	Meringue Shells* filled
	  with Fresh Fruit
		Drawn Butter
		Sparkling Borsch*
		  (appetizer)

*All starred recipes appear in these encyclopedias. See index for pages.

is plentiful enough that people often choose their foods on factors other than nutritional value. This means that the homemaker must employ her skill to plan nutritious menus that will appeal to the family, fit the budget, and be prepared in a reasonable length of time. No matter how closely you follow the Basic Four, you have failed to plan a good meal if the family refuses to eat the nutritious food because it is unattractive or unpalatable.

An attractive meal is the result of skillfully combining the table setting and the food. Although the table setting may seem necessary only as a means of serving food, a pleasing table setting greatly enhances the food's appearance. Therefore, planning the table setting should be included in meal planning. This does not mean that the table setting needs to be elaborate. In fact, usually a simple, yet pleasant, setting is more appropriate since the food should be the focal point of the meal.

It is easy to fall into the habit of considering the table setting only when guests are expected. However, make up your mind to resist this habit. The family meals will be more enjoyable if you take a little time before each meal to cover the table with a clean, colorful tablecloth, set plates and silverware neatly, and perhaps even pick a pretty rose or other fresh flowers for a centerpiece. (See also *Table Setting*.)

The color of the food is one of the most important factors in making a meal attractive. Choose a variety of colors, yet make sure that the colors are complementary. A simple garnish is one way of adding color. If the meal is drab, add some bright color. For example, when the meal includes boiled beef, dumplings, and coconut cream pudding, get away from the basic brown and white by topping the pudding with a maraschino cherry and adding peas and carrots and a parsley plate garnish.

A variety of shapes is also important for an appetizing meal. Fruits and vegetables, especially, can be served in a variety of shapes including whole, sliced, wedged, cubed, and mashed.

Casseroles and one-dish-meals are so popular that if you don't pay attention, it is easy to plan a meal containing several mixtures. So, if the main dish is a casserole, serve a gelatin square for a salad instead of a tossed salad and fresh fruit for dessert instead of a fruit compote.

Delicious meals don't just happen. They are planned to give a complementary blend of flavors and textures. Plan mouth-watering meals by keeping your family's likes and dislikes in mind and by imagining the flavor and texture of each food.

Special hints that will help you plan delicious meals include: complement a soft food with a crisp food, serve a tart food to accent bland flavors, at each meal serve only one starchy food other than bread, and serve dishes of varied temperatures but keep hot foods hot and cold foods cold. Remember that seasonings can perk up a dish, but they should not overwhelm other flavors. Although your family is bound to have a few favorite dishes, don't get into a rut and serve only these favorites. Occasionally, add variety to meals by trying a new recipe, seasoning, or food.

Homemakers sometimes tend to consider meal planning as a chore. However, if you keep the above suggestions in mind and use your imagination, you will find that it is fun to plan meals.

MEALY—Grainylike meal. Mealy potatoes are desirable for baking, mashing, or frying.

MEASURE—To determine the quantity or dimensions of something by comparing it with a standard. In cooking, a successful product depends on the accurate measurement of ingredients. Every kitchen should have measuring cups and spoons that have been calibrated according to the American Standards Association standards.

There are two types of measuring cups available—those for dry ingredients and those for liquids. Dry measuring cups are usually metal and hold the specified amount when levelly full. A set of dry measuring cups contains ¼ cup, ⅓ cup, ½ cup, and 1 cup utensils. Liquid measuring cups have a pouring lip so you won't spill the liquid. They should be glass or plastic so you can see the level of liquid.

Most measuring spoons are sold in sets of four—¼ teaspoon, ½ teaspoon, 1 teaspoon, and 1 tablespoon. These spoons hold the specified amount when levelly full.

Small amounts of liquid or dry foods are measured in measuring spoons. For dry ingredients, level off with straight edge. Remember not to pour or level ingredients over mixing bowl of other ingredients.

Measure liquids in a glass measuring cup placed on a flat surface. Bend down to read the desired mark at eye level. Special features of this type of measuring cup are a rim above the last mark and a pouring lip.

The volume of a utensil is easy to find by counting the number of cups or quarts of water needed to completely fill the utensil. If you want to know the surface area of a utensil, measure it from inside edges.

Pile dry ingredients lightly into measuring cup with spoon. Without shaking cup, level off with straight edge of spatula. Pack brown sugar in cup firmly enough so it will retain the cup shape when turned out.

Essential equipment in any kitchen includes measuring utensils—measuring spoons and both liquid (glass) and dry measuring cups. Nested cups are for measuring ¼ cup, ⅓ cup, ½ cup, and 1 cup. Use the spoons for measuring less than ¼ cup of an ingredient.

MEAT

How to identify cuts easily at the meat counter—
Cooking tips to assure flavor and tenderness.

Often regarded as central to all meal planning, meat is a nutritious food containing protein, vitamins, and minerals. This all-purpose food can be served in a wide variety of dishes including casseroles, main dishes, one-dish meals, sandwiches, side dishes, and a host of other delectable meals. In short, there is seemingly no end to the many uses for meat.

Meat, or the flesh of animals used as food, refers not only to beef, pork, lamb, and veal, but also covers game and sometimes poultry or fish. Even parts such as liver and kidney are called meat as are sausages and other processed forms.

It is taken for granted today that a handsome meat platter is a major attraction at the meal. However, it is thought that man was first a vegetarian, so the first human to sample meat must have had to summon his courage. While there were no reporters to record the event, he probably made a meal of an animal he found shortly after it had been killed. Since the man lived to tell his story, others went after meat, first by trapping, later by hunting, and eventually by domesticating animals.

How and when meat was first cooked is another event lost in the annals of time. Perhaps a piece of meat fell into the fire and when rescued, was consumed and enjoyed.

In ancient times as today man recognized that meat is a giver of life and a precious commodity. As such it has played a prominent role in man's religious life.

At various times sacred animals have been worshipped and/or sacrificed. Old Testament narratives are among the best records of these events, while the sacrificial lamb in the New Testament has special significance for Christians.

Directly and indirectly meat has had an impact on civilization and commerce. On one hand, domesticating livestock and raising crops meant that man could settle in one place rather than keep moving to search for food. On the other hand, living in towns and cities produced people whose occupations were not related to agriculture. Exploration and trade became necessary so that all could be fed and housed.

These were also the days before refrigeration. Salt and spices, besides improving the flavor of food, were important preservatives, especially for meat. Great explorers like Marco Polo and Christopher Columbus knew firsthand the value of the spices and the riches to be gained both financially and gustatorily from locating shorter routes.

The earliest settlers in the New World imported livestock. The first cattle were brought by the Spanish explorer, Hernando Cortes, early in the sixteenth century. They were introduced by way of Mexico and taken into what is now the southwestern United States. The first hog shipment on record came from Cuba in the 1530s. The first recorded shipment of sheep arrived in Virginia in 1609 and the following year, a large shipment of cattle arrived.

The Pilgrims who settled in New England brought a few cattle and hogs with them. Without that foresight, survival would have been much more difficult.

But, like their friends and neighbors back home, it was essential to have some way of holding meat for later use. The most practical method was by salting and

Sunday dinner at its best

← An old-fashioned meal includes Rolled Rump Roast with Herb Gravy, carrots and potatoes, rolls, and a meringue-topped cream pie.

"packing" it into barrels. From this process the meat "packing industry" derived its name. "Packing" is hardly an adequate term for the many functions of the modern meat industry. Its visible function is to bring meat in all forms to market, but it performs many unseen services as well. Among its many employees are research scientists who test products and create new ones and home economists who develop cooking times and procedures for various cuts designed to obtain greatest flavor, tenderness, and serving yield.

Meat is so important in the diet that it is one of the cornerstones of the Basic Four Food Groups. Two servings or more are needed daily. Meat is an excellent source of protein, B vitamins, and minerals.

Since meat is important for its high-quality protein, no study of meat is adequate without more specific information on this topic. Meat supplies what nutritionists call high-quality or complete protein. This means that all the essential amino acids, or building blocks, needed to maintain life and promote growth are present. Protein also builds muscles, repairs tissues, and helps form antibodies which are effective in fighting infection. The body can also use protein as a source of energy.

Given equal servings, the protein in one type of meat is approximately the same as the protein in every other kind. Stew meat may not have the sophistication of filet mignon, but its protein is every bit as valuable. There are nutritional differences between meats, but these differences are more in the mineral and vitamin content than in protein content. Liver, for example, is richer in vitamin A than is beef roast, and pork is an outstanding source of the B vitamin thiamine, but the protein in a serving of any meat is about the same.

How to buy

The characteristic most people want in meat is tenderness. Juiciness and flavor are in demand, too, but tenderness is most preferred in any cut of meat. King James I of England acknowledged tenderness of a fine cut by dubbing it "Sir Loyn."

How to tell in advance which cut will prove tender is a challenge to many shoppers. The meat counter is filled with an abundance of packages; precut; preweighed, and prewrapped. Ultimately, the challenge extends to the kitchen because final tenderness in a cut of meat depends upon the way it is cooked and served.

The butcher or meat cutter is seldom in sight at the market as most of his work, such as cutting and packaging, takes place behind the scenes. He is willing to help on the summons of a bell, but many shoppers are reluctant to push it just for advice on tonight's dinner selection.

In many ways, tenderness in a cut is related to the part of the animal from which it comes. Working muscles found in the leg or shoulder are less tender than muscles which play a supporting role in rib section or loin. Over the years, homemakers memorized the carcass location. Although this is still helpful, in these days of prepackaged meats, few shoppers ever see a carcass. However, they do see the bone in the cuts that they buy. Thus, identification of tender and less tender cuts by learning the shape of the bone is both easy and practical.

The Bone Shape Chart shows the five major shapes. Perhaps most familiar is the T-bone. In all four meat varieties (beef, pork, veal, and lamb) you will see the T stands for tenderness.

The rib bone, similar to the T but curved, is also found in tender cuts as is the wedge bone located in loin cuts.

The round bone indicates a leg or shoulder cut and is tender in all but beef. The blade bone, also called the 7 bone, comes from the shoulder and always means less-tender meat.

Because such a high percentage of the beef animal is made up of less tender cuts, many methods are used to make beef more tender. Less frequently are they used for other meats. Increased tenderness may be achieved mechanically by pounding, scoring, or grinding the meat before cooking. This breaks up the connective tissue. More recently tenderizers, applied commercially or at home, take effect during cooking and produce tender roasts or steaks.

In addition to the bone shape, the shopper must recognize quality in her search for tender meat. Experts use color of meat, amount of fat, and the age of the animal as guides. Bright-colored lean with a firm, fine texture is associated with top quality. The amount of marbling, those flecks of fat within the lean, is a quality factor since it enhances juiciness, flavor, and tenderness. Finally, age is important—younger animals are more tender than older ones.

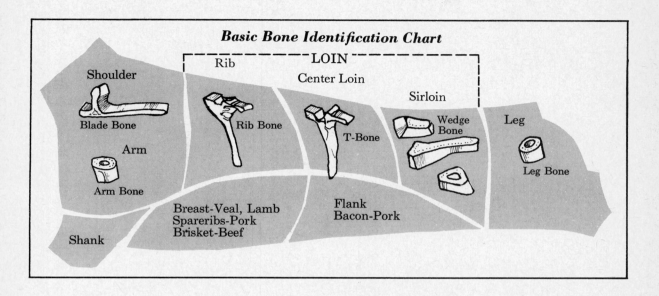

Basic Bone Identification Chart

Shoulder — Blade Bone
Arm — Arm Bone
Shank
Rib — Rib Bone
LOIN — Center Loin
T-Bone
Sirloin — Wedge Bone
Leg — Leg Bone
Breast-Veal, Lamb
Spareribs-Pork
Brisket-Beef
Flank
Bacon-Pork

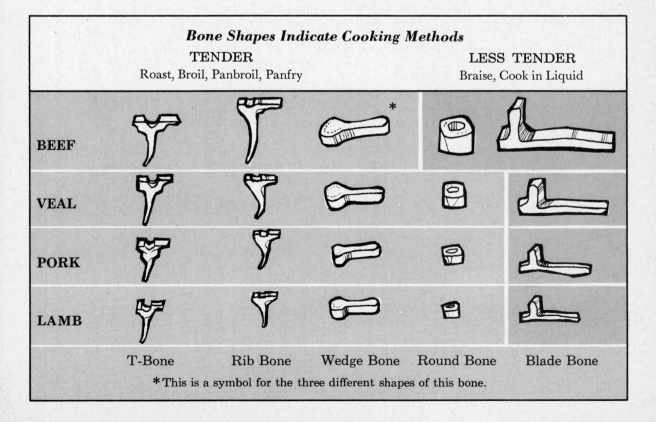

Bone Shapes Indicate Cooking Methods

	TENDER Roast, Broil, Panbroil, Panfry			LESS TENDER Braise, Cook in Liquid	
BEEF	T-Bone	Rib Bone	Wedge Bone *	Round Bone	Blade Bone
VEAL					
PORK					
LAMB					
	T-Bone	Rib Bone	Wedge Bone	Round Bone	Blade Bone

*This is a symbol for the three different shapes of this bone.

About 80 percent of the meat sold in markets has been inspected for wholesomeness in federally inspected plants. In many plants the meat is also government graded. The grade names given apply to beef, lamb, and veal. Pork is not generally merchandised according to grade since there is less variation in tenderness in pork cuts.

U. S. Prime is a grade seldom seen outside restaurants and exclusive meat shops. A very small percentage of beef receives this grade. *Choice* is the highest grade sold regularly in the retail market and in the greatest volume throughout the year. The next lower grade, *Good*, has limited availability. *Standard* and *Commercial* are lower grades not always found in the market. The two lowest grades, *Cutter* and *Canner*, are not sold in the retail meat market. Remember, however, when properly cooked, cuts from all of the grades will produce tender and delicious eating.

Meat packers also have specifications for meats which carry their company brand name. These brands may appear on the meat either instead of or in addition to one of the government grades.

The grade shield and the round federal inspection mark indicating wholesomeness are applied to the carcass at the meat packing plant. They may not show up on each individual cut in the market. If they are visible, however, they do not need to be trimmed away before cooking because an edible vegetable dye is used.

Armed with information on bone shapes and guides to quality, the shopper is ready to consider her budget both in terms of the money and preparation time available.

If the amount of money is limited, the shopper should concentrate on the less-tender cuts wearing a lower price tag. The term less tender is not a disguise for "less desirable" because the meat can be made tender and delectable through proper cooking. Many of the famous gourmet recipes begin with a less-tender cut and go on from there to develop a dish that is rich in flavor and appearance. Cooks from around the world with more imagination than money have produced such masterpieces as the ragout of France, goulash of Hungary, haggis of Scotland, chili con carne of Mexico, and stew of Ireland.

As the woman who works outside the home knows, money is not the only commodity to be budgeted. Time does not always permit a succulent stew for tonight's dinner. Ground meats can be prepared quickly and economically as can many canned meats, sausages, and cooked hams.

Vegetable–Meat Cups

1 beaten egg
¼ cup milk
¼ cup coarsely crushed saltine crackers (6 crackers)
¾ teaspoon salt
Dash pepper
½ teaspoon Worcestershire sauce
1 pound ground beef
Packaged instant mashed potatoes (enough for 4 servings)
2 tablespoons sliced green onion
½ 10¾-ounce can condensed Cheddar cheese soup (⅔ cup)
3 tablespoons milk
½ 10-ounce package frozen peas, cooked and drained

In mixing bowl combine beaten egg, milk, cracker crumbs, salt, pepper, and Worcestershire sauce. Add ground beef; mix well. On 4 squares of waxed paper shape meat mixture into 4 patties each with a 5-inch diameter. Shape each patty over an inverted 5-ounce custard cup; peel off and discard the waxed paper. Chill 1 hour.

Place the inverted cups in a shallow baking pan; bake at 375° for 20 minutes. While the meat cups are baking, prepare the mashed potatoes following package directions; stir in the sliced green onion. Lift baked meat cups from custard cups and turn upright; fill with mashed potatoes. In saucepan mix the cheese soup with 3 tablespoons milk; stir in peas. Heat, stirring occasionally. Spoon over meat. Garnish with parsley, if desired. Serves 4.

A unique meal-in-a-dish

←Vegetable-Meat Cups feature ground beef and onion-flavored potatoes. The cheese sauce, dotted with peas, starts with soup.

When the food budget is healthy, shoppers naturally gravitate to the highly prized cuts that are tender to begin with. These are the roasts, steaks, and chops to be cooked rare, medium, or well-done to suit the family's preference.

Having chosen the cut, the final decision has to do with the amount to buy. If the meat is boneless, it will furnish four servings per pound. Meat with the bone in such as pot roast, will yield about two servings per pound. Meat containing a high proportion of bone such as spareribs will provide only one serving per pound. It's best to add an extra serving or two so that the platter can go around the second time; or to plan the meat purchase so that there will be enough cooked meat to make sandwiches or other tasty leftover dishes. Many busy homemakers like to buy enough for two meals at one time and reserve half in the freezer for a bonus meal.

How to store

If storage space (refrigerator and freezer) and budget allow it, one store trip can serve many meals. Meat must be stored properly, however, as once it has passed the "point of no return" nothing will bring it back to its original freshness.

Microorganisms and enzymes are the villains in the meat spoilage story. Warm temperatures speed their work, so a refrigerator temperature near freezing is recommended. The amount of exposed surface area plays a supporting role in this drama. The more surface exposed, the greater the likelihood of contamination from outside. Thus, ground meat and meat that has been mechanically tenderized are more likely to spoil than are roasts because they offer a proportionately larger exposed surface. The organ meats such as livers and brains are also especially susceptible.

Meat that is prepackaged in transparent wrap need not be rewrapped at home for refrigerator storage. However, market paper-wrapped meat should be rewrapped loosely in waxed paper as it needs some air to "breathe" at refrigerator temperature.

Meat may be wiped with paper towels, but should not be washed. Some refrigerators have special compartments in which meat can be stored unwrapped. Lunch meat, bacon, franks and other cured meat can be stored in their original packages.

For freezer storage, meat is wrapped differently than for the refrigerator. Although the microorganisms and enzymes harmful at refrigerator temperature are inactivated at freezer temperatures of 0°F. and below, a new foe enters the scene; dehydration. His alias, "freezer burn," is better known. Best preventive measure is tight wrapping in moisture-vaporproof material, one that does not allow the package to breath. Lightweight foil and waxed paper, while useful for refrigerator storage of meat, are not an effective freezer wrap.

To prepare meat for freezing, it should be divided into amounts suitable for cooking at one time. The cutting of a large roast when frozen solid is a formidable task and one that can be avoided by forethought. The wrapping material should be pulled tightly around the meat so that a minimum of air is left inside, and the package should be sealed tightly and marked with the contents, weight, and date.

Leftover cooked meat and meat combinations such as casseroles should be cooled and refrigerated promptly. After cooling, they should be covered or wrapped loosely to prevent drying. They will hold for a day or two in the refrigerator. For freezer storage, the "tight wrap" rule holds. Cooked meat dishes can be kept in the freezer for up to two months.

It is difficult to give exact rules as to the number of days fresh meat can be stored in the refrigerator, or how many months in the freezer. This is because so many factors enter in, such as store treatment before purchase, the time it takes to get the meat from the store to the refrigerator, and the exact temperature inside the refrigerator or freezer.

Here are a few general guidelines, though. Larger roasts will store in the refrigerator for three to four days; smaller steaks and chops for three days. Ground meats and variety meats such as liver should be used within two days.

Beef, veal, and lamb roasts have a freezer life of six to eight months; pork roasts, three to six. The smaller cuts and ground meat should be used within four months.

The exception to the "longer life for larger cuts" rule is ham, as it does not freeze well for long periods.

Consequently, storage charts show the possibility of keeping ham, sausage, and bacon in the freezer for up to a month.

Fresh pork, veal and variety meats will freeze satisfactorily for up to four months.

How to cook

For most meat cookery, low to moderate heat is best. This keeps juice and flavor in the meat where they belong. It also cuts down on meat shrinkage and retains tenderness particularly in meats cooked well done. Slightly higher temperatures may be used in broiling, but the intensity is regulated by moving the pan of meat farther from the heat source.

The two major ways of cooking meat are by dry heat for tender cuts of high quality and moist heat for the less tender. With the similarities and differences in mind, meat cookery is no longer a mystery.

Dry heat—This includes roasting, oven and panbroiling, panfrying, and cooking on the open grill. Check the roasting chart in this book for the time required to cook the specific weight of each cut. Roasting charts, not as accurate as a meat thermometer, but helpful in figuring out when to start cooking, should be used only as an approximate guide to cooking time.

Oven Roasting—For best results the roast should weigh at least three pounds. The meat should be prepared for the oven allowing the roasting time shown in the chart plus another fifteen minutes for it to "set up" before carving.

The oven temperature for roasting is 325°F. The roast should be placed, fat side up, in an open pan. No water is added and no cover is used.

The roast meat thermometer is a "must" to reach the right degree of doneness. Insert the thermometer so that the tip reaches into the center of the thickest part of the roast but does not touch bone. Position the meat so the thermometer can be seen without taking the roast from the oven. When done, transfer the meat to a warm place while making gravy from the drippings.

Rolled Rump Roast

 4 pounds rolled rump roast
 ¼ teaspoon salt
   Dash pepper
 ⅛ teaspoon dried marjoram leaves, crushed
 ⅛ teaspoon dried thyme leaves, crushed
   Herb Gravy

Place meat, fat side up, on rack in shallow roasting pan. Combine salt, pepper, and herbs; rub into meat. Insert meat thermometer. Roast, uncovered, at 325° till meat thermometer registers 150° to 170°, about 2 to 2½ hours. Transfer roast to serving platter; keep warm.

Herb Gravy: Leaving crusty bits in pan, measure meat juices and fat. Skim off fat, reserving 3 tablespoons. For 2 cups gravy, return reserved fat to pan. Stir in ¼ cup all-purpose flour; cook and stir over low heat till blended. Remove pan from heat. Add water to meat juices to equal 2 cups liquid; add to pan all at once and blend. Stir in 1 tablespoon snipped parsley, ¾ teaspoon salt, and a dash *each* pepper, crushed dried marjoram leaves, and crushed dried thyme leaves. Cook and stir till bubbly. Simmer 2 to 3 minutes.

Oven Broiling—Hamburger, tender steaks, chops, and ham slices, one to two inches thick, are all good candidates for this method. Cuts less than one inch thick are better panbroiled. A tender cut is the main requirement. The second is proper use of the broiler. Follow directions that come with the range, noting especially whether the door must be left open or closed during the cooking operation.

To prepare steaks for broiling, slash the fat at the edge in several places to prevent curling. The meat should be put on the broiler rack and the rack set three to five inches from the source of heat. Turn only once during cooking. Season with salt and pepper before serving.

Panbroiling—Thinner cuts of tender meat may be panbroiled in a heavy skillet which has been rubbed with a little fat to prevent sticking. After heating the skillet, brown the meat on one side; then turn and brown the other. Reduce heat and keep

Meat Roasting Chart

Place the meat with fat side up, on a rack in a low-sided open roasting pan. Do not add water and do not cover the meat. Insert a roast meat thermometer so that the tip reaches into the center of the thickest muscle. Roast the meat at a constant oven temperature of 325° unless otherwise indicated on the chart.

Although the thickness of the meat and its overall shape influence how fast the roast cooks, the schedules suggested below, based on total weight, provide guidelines in judging how much time to allow for roasting. The meat thermometer registers internal temperature and tells when the meat has reached the desired doneness.

Cut	Approximate Weight (Pounds)	Internal Temp. on Removal from Oven	Approximate Cooking Time (Total Time)
Beef			
Standing Rib	4 to 6	140°F. (rare) 160°F. (medium) 170°F. (well done)	2¼ to 2¾ hrs. 2¾ to 3¼ hrs. 3¼ to 3½ hrs.
Standing Rib	6 to 8	140°F. (rare) 160°F. (medium) 170°F. (well done)	2¾ to 3 hrs. 3 to 3½ hrs. 3¾ to 4 hrs.
Rolled Rib	5 to 7	140°F. (rare) 160°F. (medium) 170°F. (well done)	3¼ to 3½ hrs. 3¾ to 4 hrs. 4½ to 4¾ hrs.
Rolled Rump	4 to 6	150°F. to 170°F.	2 to 2½ hrs.
Sirloin Tip	3½ to 4	150°F. to 170°F.	2 to 2¾ hrs.
Rib Eye or Delmonico (Roast at 350°F.)	4 to 6	140°F. (rare) 160°F. (medium) 170°F. (well done)	1½ to 1¾ hrs. 1¾ hrs. 2 hrs.
Tenderloin, whole (Roast at 425°F.)	4 to 6	140°F. (rare)	45 min. to 1 hr.
Tenderloin, half (Roast at 425°F.)	2 to 3	140°F. (rare)	45 to 50 min.
Veal			
Leg	5 to 8	170°F.	2¾ to 3¾ hrs.
Loin	4 to 6	170°F.	2½ to 3 hrs.
Rolled Shoulder	4 to 6	170°F.	3½ to 3¾ hrs.
Lamb			
Leg, whole	5 to 8	175°F. to 180°F.	3½ to 3¾ hrs.
Leg, half	3 to 4	175°F. to 180°F.	3 to 3½ hrs.
Square Cut Shoulder	4 to 6	175°F. to 180°F.	2½ to 3 hrs.
Rolled Shoulder	3 to 5	175°F. to 180°F.	2¾ to 3 hrs.

Meat Roasting Chart			
Cut	Approximate Weight (Pounds)	Internal Temp. on Removal from Oven	Approximate Cooking Time (Total Time)
Fresh Pork			
Loin, center	3 to 5	170°F.	2½ to 3 hrs.
Loin, center; rolled	3 to 4	170°F.	2½ to 3 hrs.
Loin, half	5 to 7	170°F.	3½ to 4¼ hrs.
Loin, blade or sirloin	3 to 4	170°F.	2¼ to 2¾ hrs.
Boston Shoulder	4 to 6	170°F.	3 to 4 hrs.
Boston Shoulder Roll	3 to 5	170°F.	2 to 3 hrs.
Leg (fresh ham)	12 to 16	170°F.	5 to 6 hrs.
Leg, half (fresh ham)	5 to 7	170°F.	3½ to 4½ hrs.
Cured and Smoked Pork			
Ham (cook before eating)			
whole	10 to 14	160°F.	3½ to 4 hrs.
half	5 to 7	160°F.	2½ to 3 hrs.
shank or butt	3 to 4	160°F.	2 to 2¼ hrs.
Ham (fully cooked)			
whole	10 to 14	130°F.	2½ to 3 hrs.
half	5 to 7	130°F.	1¾ to 2¼ hrs.
whole, boneless	8 to 10	130°F.	2 to 2¼ hrs.
half, boneless	4 to 5	130°F.	1½ to 2 hrs.
Picnic Shoulder (cook before eating)	5 to 8	170°F.	3 to 4 hrs.

turning meat as needed to cook it evenly. The pan should not be covered nor moisture added. Season the meat and serve it hot.

Panfrying—This method is best for thin cuts lacking in natural fat such as round steak and liver. Moderate rather than high heat should be used to prevent drying out the surface of the meat. Sautéing is a form of panfrying.

Barbecuing or Grilling—Outdoor chefs feel that fresh air adds allure to a good steak or improves an average one. Ground meats and cuts tender enough for broiling work well on the outdoor grill. Less-tender cuts such as bottom round, chuck, and flank steak are satisfactory, too, with a bit of tenderizing beforehand.

Lamb and Frank Burgers

⅓ cup milk
⅔ cup soft bread crumbs
¼ cup chopped green pepper
¼ cup chopped onion
1 tablespoon Worcestershire sauce
¾ teaspoon salt
1½ pounds ground lamb
4 to 5 frankfurters, diced
8 hamburger buns, split and toasted

Combine first 6 ingredients. Add meats; mix well. Shape into 8 patties, ½ inch thick. Grill over *medium* coals 8 to 10 minutes. Turn; grill 6 to 8 minutes. Serve in buns. Serves 8.

Meat Seasoning Guide

Start by adding ¼ teaspoon of a dried herb or a dash to ⅛ teaspoon of a ground spice for each 4 servings. (See *Herb*, *Spice* for additional information.)

Herbs and Spices	Meat				
	Beef	Veal	Ham	Lamb	Pork
Allspice	*		*	*	
Basil	*	*		*	*
Bay Leaf	*	*		*	
Caraway Seed	*			*	*
Celery Seed	*				
Chili Powder	*				
Cloves			*		*
Cumin	*				
Curry	*	*		*	
Dill				*	
Garlic	*			*	*
Ginger	*	*	*	*	*
Mace	*	*			
Marjoram	*	*		*	*
Mint		*		*	
Mustard	*	*	*		*
Oregano	*	*		*	*
Rosemary	*	*		*	*
Saffron					
Sage		*		*	*
Savory	*	*		*	*
Tarragon	*				
Thyme	*	*		*	*

Moist heat—The combination of slow cooking and moist heat can transform a budget-priced cut into rich eating. The methods used are called braising, and cooking in liquid.

Braising—Less-tender roasts of beef and lamb benefit from braising. The combination of heat and moisture softens the meat fibers and connective tissue. Pork, veal cutlets, and other lean cuts need moist heat to prevent their drying out.

The meat may or may not be dipped in seasoned flour, then browned in a small amount of fat in a heavy pan that can be covered. After browning, a little water or other liquid is added and the pan covered. Very slow surface heat or a 325° to 350° F. oven will complete the cooking. Braising a roast is also called "pot roasting."

When preparing stews, the meat is cut into cubes before adding the liquid and seasonings. A flavorful stew is as simple or as fancy as desired.

German Beef Stew

    1½ pounds beef stew meat, cut
        in 1-inch cubes
      2 tablespoons salad oil
      1 large apple, peeled and shredded
      1 medium carrot, shredded
      ½ onion, sliced
      ½ cup water
      ⅓ cup dry red wine
      ½ teaspoon anchovy paste
      1 clove garlic, minced
      2 beef bouillon cubes
      1 small bay leaf
      ⅛ teaspoon dried thyme leaves,
        crushed
      4 teaspoons cornstarch
      ¼ cup cold water
      ¼ teaspoon Kitchen Bouquet
      4 cups medium noodles, cooked
      ¼ teaspoon poppy seed

Brown meat in hot oil. Add next 10 ingredients. Cover and cook over low heat till beef is tender, about 2 hours. Remove bay leaf. Combine cornstarch and ¼ cup cold water; add to beef mixture. Cook and stir till thickened. Stir in Kitchen Bouquet. Serve over drained noodles sprinkled with poppy seed. Makes 4 servings.

Cooking in liquid: In the "good old days" this was called "boiling," but if the water boils, the meat won't be as tender as if a lower, simmering temperature is used. As a cooking method it is related to braising, but larger quantities of liquid are used, and it is usually reserved for whole cuts such as beef brisket. Variety meats such as tongue or chitterlings are cooked in liquid too. Sometimes, vegetables or greens are added to the liquid towards the end of the long, slow cooking time.

Although moist heat cooking in all its forms is necessary for less-tender cuts, this is not the only reason homemakers put it to use. Frequently tender pork, lamb, or veal roasts and chops cut from young, lean animals have very little surface fat covering or internal marbling. Some moisture in a covered pan is needed to keep the meat from drying out. This technique is particularly important when the chops are cut less than one inch thick.

Cranberry Pork Chops

    4 pork chops, cut ¾ inch thick
    1 8½-ounce can pineapple slices
    ½ cup whole cranberry sauce
    1 chicken bouillon cube
    ½ cup boiling water
    2 tablespoons brown sugar
    2 tablespoons vinegar
    1 green pepper, cut in 1-inch
        pieces
    2 tablespoons cornstarch
    2 tablespoons cold water

Trim fat from chops. In skillet cook trimmings till about 1 tablespoon fat accumulates; discard trimmings. Brown chops. Season with a little salt and pepper. Drain pineapple, reserving syrup; add syrup to chops with cranberry sauce.

Dissolve bouillon cube in the boiling water; add to chops along with brown sugar and vinegar. Cover skillet and simmer till chops are tender, about 40 minutes. Add pineapple and green pepper; cover and cook 10 minutes more. Remove chops and pineapple to warm platter.

Combine the cornstarch and the 2 tablespoons water; stir into cranberry mixture in the skillet. Cook and stir till thickened and bubbly. Pour sauce over chops. Makes 4 servings.

Veal Parmesan Supper

    ¼ cup fine dry bread crumbs
    ¼ cup grated Parmesan cheese
    ½ teaspoon salt
        Dash pepper
    ½ teaspoon garlic salt
    ½ teaspoon paprika
    4 veal chops, ¾ inch thick
    1 beaten egg
    3 tablespoons olive or salad oil
    4 medium potatoes, peeled and
        quartered
    1 8-ounce can tomato sauce
    1 teaspoon dried oregano leaves,
        crushed
    4 thin slices mozzarella cheese

Combine crumbs, Parmesan, and seasonings. Dip chops in egg, then in crumbs. Brown slowly in hot oil; arrange potatoes around meat. Combine tomato sauce, 1 cup water, and oregano. Pour over meat and potatoes.

Cover; simmer till meat and potatoes are done, 45 to 50 minutes. Last few minutes place cheese slice atop each chop. Serves 4.

Another reason for the popularity of braised meats is the delectable sauces in which they are cooked. Juices from the meat mingle with seasonings and liquid. Besides water, tomato juice, pineapple juice, canned soups, or wines lend special goodness to the finished dishes.

What fine perfume does for grooming, herbs and spices do for cooking. They elevate a good dish into an elegant one. Use the Meat Seasoning Guide to see which seasonings harmonize well with a particular meat.

A well-browned, artfully seasoned roast or meat loaf is a joy to behold and serve. However, occasionally you will notice a slightly reddish color along the surface of the cooked meat. This occurs when the nitrates and nitrites naturally present in cooking liquids, celery, onions, and other seasonings react with the meat. The line of color, though puzzling, is harmless.

Perhaps nothing wins more compliments at the dinner table than does the meat course. By following the basics of buymanship and meat cookery, even beginners in the kitchen can do themselves proud.

MEATBALL—A mixture of ground meat and ingredients such as bread crumbs and seasonings shaped into balls before cooking.

Even-sized meatballs are easy to shape if you pat the meat mixture into a rectangle on waxed paper, then cut it into squares. Gently roll each square into a ball.

Even though you shape perfectly rounded meatballs, they often become flattened during cooking. To avoid this, brown only a few meatballs at a time and gently, yet continuously, shake the skillet back and forth over the heat. (See also *Ground Beef.*)

For perfectly round meatballs, wet hands slightly, then make the balls by gently rolling the meat mixture between your hands.

When browning meatballs, cook a few at a time and shake the skillet gently to promote even browning and help keep the balls round.

Cherry-Sauced Ham Balls

  1 beaten egg
  3 tablespoons milk
  ⅓ cup fine dry bread crumbs
  1½ pounds ground fully cooked ham
  2 tablespoons shortening
         . . .
  1 21-ounce can cherry pie filling
  1 tablespoon lemon juice
  ½ teaspoon ground cinnamon
    Dash ground cloves

Combine egg, milk, bread crumbs, and dash pepper. Add ham; mix well. Shape into 18 balls. Brown balls in hot shortening, shaking pan often to keep balls round. Drain off fat. Add ¼ cup water. Simmer, covered, 15 to 20 minutes, turning balls occasionally. Meanwhile, heat pie filling, 2 tablespoons water, lemon juice, cinnamon, and cloves. Spoon some sauce atop balls; pass remainder. Serves 6.

Saucy Italian Meatballs

For sauce, cook ¾ cup chopped onion and 1 clove garlic, minced, in 3 tablespoons hot salad oil till tender but not brown. Stir in two 16-ounce cans tomatoes, cut up; two 6-ounce cans tomato paste (1⅓ cups); 2 cups water; 1½ teaspoons dried oregano leaves, crushed; 1½ teaspoons salt; 1 teaspoon sugar; ½ teaspoon pepper; and 1 bay leaf. Simmer, uncovered, for 30 minutes; remove bay leaf.

Meanwhile, soak 4 slices bread in ½ cup water 2 to 3 minutes. Add 2 eggs, mixing well. Combine with 1 pound ground beef; ¼ cup grated Parmesan cheese; 2 tablespoons snipped parsley; 1 teaspoon salt; ¼ teaspoon dried oregano leaves, crushed; and dash pepper. With wet hands, form into small balls (about 24). Brown slowly in 2 tablespoons hot salad oil. Add meatballs to sauce; simmer, loosely covered, for 30 minutes. Serve over hot cooked spaghetti. Pass extra Parmesan cheese. Serves 6.

Company fare

Cherry-Sauced Ham Balls are elegant, yet→ easy. The meatballs take only four ingredients and the sauce uses canned pie filling.

Meatball Heroes

2 tablespoons salad oil
½ clove garlic, minced
½ envelope onion soup mix (¼ cup)
1 8-ounce can tomato sauce
1 teaspoon sugar
½ teaspoon dried oregano leaves,
    crushed
1 pound ground beef
½ cup milk
⅓ cup fine dry bread crumbs
2 tablespoons salad oil
8 frankfurter buns, split and
    toasted

In saucepan heat together the first 2 tablespoons oil and garlic; stir in soup mix, 1 cup water, tomato sauce, sugar, and oregano. Gently boil sauce, uncovered, 10 to 15 minutes, stirring occasionally till slightly thickened.

Combine meat, milk, bread crumbs, ½ teaspoon salt, and dash pepper. Shape in 24 small balls. Brown in the 2 tablespoons oil. Add to sauce; cover and cook for about 20 minutes. Arrange 3 meatballs on bottom half of *each* frankfurter bun. Spoon on a little sauce; cover with bun top. Makes 8 servings.

MEAT GLAZE—1. Juices lost by meat as it cooks. These concentrated juices give a meat flavor to gravies and sauces. 2. A mixture brushed or poured on the surface of meat to give the meat a glossy look.

Jewel Glaze

In saucepan combine one 10-ounce jar currant jelly, ½ cup light corn syrup, ½ teaspoon grated lemon peel, ¼ cup lemon juice, ¼ teaspoon ground cloves, ¼ teaspoon ground cinnamon, and ¼ teaspoon ground allspice. Bring to boiling over low heat. Remove from heat. Stir in 8 ounces chopped mixed candied fruits and peels. Last 30 minutes, spoon on glaze; baste occasionally. Makes 2 cups.

MEAT LOAF—A mixture of ground meat and other ingredients, such as eggs, bread crumbs, onion, and seasonings, shaped into a loaf or ring, then baked.

Speed up meat loaf mixing by using the one bowl method. Combine egg, liquid, and dry ingredients, then gently mix in meat.

Although ground beef is the most popular meat used in meat loaves, it is by no means the only suitable meat. Ground ham, veal, and pork are equally as tasty. A meat loaf made with a mixture of ground meats offers a delightful flavor combination.

Many people associate meat loaf with leftovers and plain meals. Actually, with a little imagination and special ingredients, such as wine and mushrooms, a meat loaf can become a gourmet entrée.

One easy way to make a meat loaf special is to glaze it. Use a simple mixture of catsup, brown sugar, and seasonings or more unusual ingredients such as jelly, jam, fruit juice, and corn syrup. Occasional basting during the latter part of the cooking period produces a glossy finish.

Whether you use a prepared food, such as a can of cheese soup, or concoct a subtly flavored wine-mushroom sauce from scratch, a sauce is certain to dress up any meat loaf. Either spoon the sauce over the entire loaf before serving or let each person spoon sauce onto his own portion.

Glazed meat loaf

Use the center of this meat loaf ring as a → serving dish for vegetables. Glazed Ham Ring is heaped full with creamed peas and potatoes.

Handle the meat loaf gently as you shape it in the baking dish. Too much handling makes the loaf undesirably compact.

Twin Meat Loaves

A flavorful combination of beef and pork—

        3 cups soft bread cubes (about
            4 slices cut in ½-inch cubes)
        ¾ cup milk
        2 eggs
                . . .
    1½ pounds ground beef
        ½ pound ground pork
        ¼ cup finely chopped onion
        ¼ cup finely chopped celery
        1 tablespoon Worcestershire sauce
    1½ teaspoons salt
        ½ teaspoon poultry seasoning
        ⅛ teaspoon pepper
                . . .
        ¼ cup chili sauce *or* ¼ cup
            catsup and 2 tablespoons
            corn syrup

Soak bread cubes in milk. Add eggs; beat with rotary beater. Add ground beef, ground pork, onion, celery, Worcestershire sauce, salt, poultry seasoning, and pepper; mix thoroughly. Form into 2 loaves. Place in 13x9x2-inch baking pan. Bake, uncovered, at 350° for 1 hour.

For glaze, spread both meat loaves with chili sauce *or* spread with a mixture of the catsup and corn syrup. Bake the meat loaves 15 minutes longer. Makes 8 to 10 servings.

Midas Meat Loaf

        1 celery heart, about 2½ inches
            in diameter
        1 cup grated sharp Cheddar cheese
        2 tablespoons finely chopped
            canned pimiento
        3 pounds ground beef
        ½ cup quick-cooking rolled oats
        ½ cup evaporated milk
        1 tablespoon seasoned salt
        1 teaspoon garlic powder
        1 teaspoon Worcestershire sauce
        ½ teaspoon chili powder
        ⅛ teaspoon liquid smoke
        2 slightly beaten eggs
        ½ cup chopped green onion
        ¼ cup chopped green pepper
        1 pound sliced bacon

Remove celery leaves and cut celery heart to about 8 or 9 inches long; wash and dry. Keep bottom of celery heart intact; do not remove root. Gently pull branches apart; sprinkle with salt. Combine cheese and pimiento; spread generously between celery branches. Wrap tightly in foil; chill while preparing meat loaf.

Combine ground beef, rolled oats, evaporated milk, seasoned salt, garlic powder, Worcestershire sauce, chili powder, ½ teaspoon pepper, liquid smoke, eggs, green onion, and green pepper; mix. Turn meat mixture out onto a large sheet of waxed paper and pat out to an oval about 12x11x¾ inches. Cut off only the *very bottom of root* of celery heart; place celery on center of meat. Fold the meat up and over celery. Pat into roll shape, completely enclosing the cheese- and pimento-filled celery.

Lay bacon slices in chevron pattern over top of meat roll, making sure that slices overlap slightly. Gently lift roll on one side and tuck bacon ends underneath. Repeat on other side. Use wooden picks to hold bacon ends in place, if necessary. Tie roll securely with string, but not so tightly as to cut the roll. Wrap in foil; seal top with drugstore fold, but do not close ends of the aluminum foil roll.

Insert spit through center of celery and balance; close ends of foil around spit. Using a line of *hot* coals on each side of roll and drip pan underneath, let meat rotate 1¼ hours. Remove foil and cook 20 minutes longer. Slice to serve, removing strings and wooden picks as you carve. Makes 10 to 12 servings.

Ham–Rice Loaves

⅓ cup uncooked long-grain rice
2 beaten eggs
¾ cup milk
½ cup finely chopped onion
½ teaspoon salt
1 pound ground fully cooked ham
    (3 cups)
1 pound ground veal
    Paprika
1 tablespoon instant minced onion
¼ cup milk
1 cup dairy sour cream
2 tablespoons prepared mustard

Cook long-grain rice according to package directions. Combine eggs, ¾ cup milk, cooked rice, chopped onion, salt, and dash pepper. Add ground ham and ground veal; mix well. Pat mixture into six 4½x2¾x2¼-inch loaf pans *or* one 9x5x3-inch loaf pan. Sprinkle with paprika. Bake at 350° for 40 to 45 minutes for small loaves or 1½ hours for large loaf.

To prepare sauce, soften instant minced onion in ¼ cup milk. In small saucepan stir onion and milk into the sour cream. Add prepared mustard. Heat and stir over low heat (*do not boil*). Serve with loaves. Serves 6.

Glazed Ham Ring

1½ pounds ground fully cooked ham
1¼ pounds ground pork
2 beaten eggs
1½ cups soft bread crumbs
½ cup chopped onion
½ cup milk
½ cup brown sugar
1 tablespoon prepared mustard
2 tablespoons vinegar
1 tablespoon water

Thoroughly combine ground ham, ground pork, eggs, soft bread crumbs, chopped onion, and milk. Press mixture into a lightly oiled 6-cup ring mold. Invert on shallow baking pan; remove mold. Bake at 350° for 1¼ hours.

Meanwhile, to prepare glaze, blend brown sugar and prepared mustard. Stir in vinegar and water. During last 30 minutes of baking time, spoon glaze over ham ring. Baste with glaze 3 or 4 times. Makes 8 to 10 servings.

Spicy Ham Loaf

Drain one 29-ounce jar spiced peach halves, reserving ½ cup syrup. Arrange, cut side up, in bottom of 9x5x3-inch loaf pan. Combine reserved syrup, 1 pound ground fully cooked ham, 1 pound ground fresh pork, 1 cup soft bread crumbs, 2 eggs, 3 tablespoons chili sauce, 2 tablespoons vinegar, and 1 teaspoon dry mustard. Mix well; press over peaches. Bake at 350° for 1¼ to 1½ hours.

Drain off excess juices; carefully invert meat loaf on serving platter. Stud peaches with whole cloves; sprinkle with brown sugar. Bake 5 minutes. Makes 6 to 8 servings.

Favorite Beef Loaf

1½ pounds ground beef
½ cup medium cracker crumbs
2 beaten eggs
1 8-ounce can tomato sauce
¼ cup finely chopped onion
2 tablespoons chopped green
    pepper
1 teaspoon salt
    Dash dried thyme leaves,
    crushed
    Dash dried marjoram leaves,
    crushed

Combine ground beef, medium cracker crumbs, beaten eggs, tomato sauce, finely chopped onion, chopped green pepper, salt, thyme, and marjoram; mix well. Shape meat mixture into loaf in an 11¾x7½x1¾-inch baking dish. Bake at 350° about 1¼ hours. Serves 6 to 8.

Cranberry Meat Loaves

In mixing bowl thoroughly combine 1 pound ground beef, 1 cup cooked rice, ½ cup tomato juice, 1 slightly beaten egg, ¼ cup minced onion, 1 tablespoon Kitchen Bouquet, and 1½ teaspoons salt. Shape meat mixture into 5 loaves. Place in 13½x8¾x1¾-inch baking dish.

Combine 1 16-ounce can whole cranberry sauce, ⅓ cup brown sugar, and 1 tablespoon lemon juice; spoon over meat loaves. Bake at 350° for 40 minutes. Remove meat loaves to warm serving platter. Pour cranberry sauce into gravy boat; serve with meat. Serves 5.

MEAT PATTY—A flattened cake of ground meat. Ingredients such as egg and bread crumbs are often added to stretch the meat and give flavor. (See also *Ground Beef.*)

Ham Patties

Combine 2 cups ground fully cooked ham, ½ cup soft bread crumbs; ¼ cup chopped green onion, ⅓ cup milk, 1 slightly beaten egg, and dash pepper. Shape into 4 patties. Brown slowly in hot shortening. Heat and stir 1 cup dairy sour cream just till hot. Top patties with sour cream and a few snipped green onion tops. Makes 4 servings.

Beef Patties Parmesan

Combine 1 pound ground beef; ½ cup packaged biscuit mix; ⅓ cup tomato juice; ¼ cup finely chopped green pepper; 1 slightly beaten egg; 1 small clove garlic, minced; 1 teaspoon salt; ½ teaspoon dried oregano leaves, crushed; ½ teaspoon Worcestershire sauce; and dash pepper. Mix lightly till ingredients are blended.

Shape into 4 patties; place in greased shallow baking pan. Bake at 400° for 20 minutes. Remove from oven; sprinkle each patty with shredded Parmesan cheese and garnish with sliced pimiento-stuffed green olives. Serve on hot buttered noodles. Serves 4.

Roast Beef Patties

¼ cup chopped onion
3 tablespoons butter or margarine
¼ cup all-purpose flour
½ cup milk
2 cups ground cooked roast beef
2 tablespoons snipped parsley
1 tablespoon chili sauce
¼ teaspoon salt
1 beaten egg
2 tablespoons water
⅓ cup fine dry bread crumbs
2 tablespoons butter or margarine
    Mushroom Sauce

In skillet cook onion in 3 tablespoons butter or margarine; blend in all-purpose flour. Add milk; cook, stirring constantly, till bubbly. Remove from heat. Blend in beef, parsley, chili sauce, and salt. Chill thoroughly.

Shape into 6 to 8 patties. Mix egg with water. Dip patties in egg, then in crumbs. Brown in 2 tablespoons butter or margarine. Serve with Mushroom Sauce. Makes 4 servings.

Mushroom Sauce: In saucepan cook ¼ cup chopped onion and ¼ cup chopped green pepper in 1 tablespoon butter or margarine till tender. Add one 10½-ounce can condensed cream of mushroom soup; one 3-ounce can chopped mushrooms, drained and finely chopped; ⅓ cup milk; and dash pepper. Cook and stir until heated through.

For uniform meat patties, gently shape the ground meat into a roll on waxed paper. Then, cut patties about ½ to ¾ inch thick.

Reduce sticking by sprinkling salt in the hot skillet before adding meat patties. The salt also helps season the meat.

Luncheon guests will be delighted with this Deviled Ham Pie.
The ham and mushroom filling is sandwiched between pastry.
Asparagus spears and cheese sauce complete this meat pie.

MEAT PIE—A main dish made of meat, usually chopped or ground, and vegetables topped with a crust of pastry, biscuits, or mashed potatoes. Leftovers seem like a new dish when you use them to make a meat pie.

Deviled Ham Pie

Prepare 1 stick piecrust mix according to package directions. Divide dough in half. Roll out one half on lightly floured surface to 7-inch circle. Trim with pastry wheel or knife. Place on *ungreased* baking sheet.

Spread with one 4½-ounce can deviled ham to within ½ inch of edge. Top with one 3-ounce can chopped mushrooms, drained. Roll remaining pastry to 7-inch circle; trim. Place over filling; crimp edges. Prick top with fork. Bake at 425° till lightly browned, 15 minutes.

Cook one 10-ounce package frozen asparagus spears according to package directions, omitting the salt from cooking water. Drain.

Combine one 11-ounce can condensed Cheddar cheese soup and ¼ cup milk; heat. Transfer pie to plate. Arrange asparagus spears on top in spoke-fashion. Cut in wedges and top with cheese sauce. Makes 4 servings.

Beef Potpie

Brown 2 pounds boneless beef stew meat *or* chuck, cut in 1-inch cubes, in small amount of hot shortening. Add 1 onion, sliced; 1 clove garlic; 1 bay leaf; 1 tablespoon salt; 1 teaspoon sugar; 1 teaspoon Worcestershire sauce; ½ teaspoon paprika; and ¼ teaspoon pepper. Pour in 3 cups water. Cover; simmer 1½ hours, stirring occasionally. Remove bay leaf and garlic.

Add 6 carrots, cut in 2-inch lengths; 6 small potatoes, peeled and halved; and 6 small onions. Cover and cook 30 minutes longer. Add 1 cup frozen peas *or* drained canned peas; continue cooking till meat and vegetables are tender, about 10 minutes. Remove from heat; skim fat.

Put ½ cup cold water in shaker; add ¼ cup all-purpose flour. Shake well; slowly stir into stew. Return stew to heat; cook and stir till thickened. Season to taste. Cook and stir 5 minutes more. Pour into casserole dish; top with Biscuits. Bake at 450° till biscuits are done, about 12 to 15 minutes. Serves 6 to 8.

Biscuits: Sift together 2 cups sifted all-purpose flour, 4 teaspoons baking powder, 2 teaspoons sugar, ½ teaspoon salt, and ½ teaspoon cream of tartar. Cut in ½ cup shortening till like coarse crumbs. Add ⅔ cup milk all at once; stir only till dough follows fork. On lightly floured surface knead gently ½ minute. Roll ½ inch thick. Cut with floured 1½-inch cutter. Arrange atop *hot* stew.

Awe guests and family alike by serving Flaming Pears Melba. The combination of pears with a cream cheese-walnut filling and bright red raspberry sauce is delightfully delicious.

MEAT TENDERIZER—Any method or substance that breaks down the connective tissue of meat, making it easier to cut or chew.

The tenderizing methods most commonly used are pounding the meat with a hammerlike utensil, marinating the meat, and applying a commercial compound which contains enzymes often from the papaya that soften the protein of the connective tissue in meat.

Saucy Steak Sandwich

    1 8-ounce can tomato sauce
    ⅓ cup bottled steak sauce
    2 tablespoons brown sugar
    1 tablespoon salad oil
    6 slices French bread, cut 1
        inch thick
    1 pound round steak, cut ¼ inch
        thick
    Instant meat tenderizer

To prepare sauce combine tomato sauce, steak sauce, brown sugar, and salad oil in small saucepan. Bring to boiling. Keep warm.

Toast the slices of French bread on both sides. Cut round steak into 6 pieces. Apply instant meat tenderizer according to label directions. Preheat griddle to 400°; grease lightly. Grill meat 2 to 3 minutes on each side. Sprinkle with pepper. To serve, dip toast quickly in sauce; top with steak. Spoon on more sauce. Serves 6.

MÉLANGE *(mā länzh')*—1. A beverage made of coffee and cream and generously topped with whipped cream. 2. A preserve made of a mixture of various fruits and sugar.

MELBA SAUCE—A raspberry dessert sauce. This sweet sauce is delicious served over ice cream, pudding, or fruit.

Melba Sundaes

    Canned peach halves, chilled
    Vanilla ice cream
    Canned raspberry topping

Fill peach halves with vanilla ice cream. Top with raspberry topping from a jar.

Flaming Pears Melba

An elegant dessert—

Drain two 29-ounce cans pear halves, reserving syrup. Place 12 pear halves, cut-side down, on paper toweling; use remaining pears another time. Combine one 3-ounce package cream cheese, softened; 1 tablespoon sugar; and enough reserved syrup for spreading. Stir in ¼ cup chopped walnuts. Spread 1 tablespoon cheese mixture on flat surface of each pear. Press halves together, making 6 whole pears.

For sauce, blend ¼ cup cold water and 1 tablespoon cornstarch in saucepan; stir in one 10-ounce package frozen raspberries, thawed. Cook, stirring constantly, till thick; sieve.

Preheat ¼ cup brandy; pour atop warm raspberry sauce; ignite with long match. Immediately spoon over pears. Makes 6 servings.

MELBA TOAST—A very thin bread slice slowly heated in the oven till crisp and brown. It is named for Dame Nellie Melba, an early nineteenth-century opera singer, who ate this toast as part of her diet. Today, melba toast is used for appetizers and canapés as well as for dietary purposes.

Melba Toast

Slice bread ⅛ inch thick; trim off crusts. Place on rack above cookie sheet. Bake at 250° till toast curls and is golden brown.

Parmesan Melba Toast

Slice French bread very thin, about ¼ inch thick. Spread bread with softened butter or margarine; sprinkle with shredded Parmesan cheese. Place on rack over a cookie sheet. Bake at 325° till very crispy, about 20 minutes.

MELILOT *(mel' uh lot')*—A type of clover that is used as an herb. Sapsago cheese is flavored with melilot. (See also *Herb*.)

MELLORINE—A commercially frozen dessert that resembles ice cream or ice milk but is made with a fat other than milk fat.

MELON

Imaginative, yet practical methods for choosing and using this succulent, sweet fruit.

Few fruits have enjoyed greater world-wide popularity than have melons. These round, semitropical fruits have been favorites of a great many people—Egyptians, Greeks, Chinese, Europeans, South Americans, and North Americans—for centuries.

Melons belong to the gourd family and are divided into two distinct groups—muskmelons and watermelons. Melons of both fruit groups develop on low, trailing vines and are identified by hard rinds and soft, succulent interiors that contain a multitude of seeds. Muskmelon seeds are contained within the central cavity of the melon. Watermelons, on the other hand, have no cavities; the seeds are distributed throughout the fleshy part of the melon.

The most probable place of origin for muskmelons appears to be Asia even though most of the surviving writings and art treasures that refer to muskmelons allude to their existence and use in the Middle East. Egyptian tomb illustrations drawn about 2400 B.C. depict these flavorful fruits. Assyrians grew muskmelons around 2100 B.C., and carvings of feast tables show their use at such celebrations.

Later civilizations also refer to melon-like fruits. The Greeks and Romans undoubtedly grew them. The Greeks used muskmelons for their supposed medicinal value. The Roman author Pliny refers to the accidental development of a round, golden fruit that he called *melopepo*. This is one ancestor of today's muskmelon.

Melon monarchy

← Melon Balls Melba crowns a variety of melons—crenshaws and cantaloupe in front; honeydew and cantaloupe in back.

Records indicate that from 1400 to 1600 A.D. muskmelon cultivation spread to Europe and America. Muskmelons were common in Spain during this time. Charles VIII of France is credited with bringing them to his country. In the Western Hemisphere, various Indian tribes and settlers in South America, Mexico, and the United States also initiated melon cultivation. By the middle of the 1600s, muskmelons were becoming more widespread throughout America.

Watermelons followed a similar timetable of development except that wild watermelons first grew in Africa. Their use then spread to Europe, the Near East, and finally to America. Over the years, American ethnic groups have given watermelons many names in many languages. (See *Watermelon* for additional information.)

How melons are produced: Muskmelons and watermelons are similarly cultivated. Although some early-maturing varieties have been developed in recent years, most melon plants require a fairly long, frost-free growing season. The melons are harvested by hand when they are mature, then they are quickly graded. Refrigeration of the fruits usually follows to assure that top quality is maintained during the subsequent shipping and marketing.

In the late 1800s commercial cultivation and shipping of melons, cantaloupes in particular, were taking place in Alma, Illinois, and Rocky Ford, Colorado. Today, the production centers have vastly widened. California is the major producing state for muskmelons, but large quantities of them are also grown in Arizona, Arkansas, Colorado, Georgia, Maryland, New Jersey, and North Carolina. Watermelons are produced in every southern state.

Melon etymology

Tracing a word back to its ancestral language often discloses why the word was chosen to describe that item. For example, the word melon is a shortened form of the Greek word *meleopepon*. The Greeks coined this term from their word for apple *melon* and edible gourd *pepon*. Muskmelon probably got its name because of its fragrant aroma. The word is derived from the Persian word *musk* which means perfume.

Nutritional value: The high water content of melons makes them low in calories (about 30 calories for a 3½-ounce serving), yet they are an important source of vitamins and minerals, the proportions of which vary with the type of melon. Cantaloupes are good sources of vitamins A and C. Honeydew melons, on the other hand, contribute fair amounts of vitamin C, while watermelons provide some vitamin A.

Types of melons

Of the two major melon groups, muskmelon is probably the most diverse and includes both net-skinned varieties and the smooth-skinned varieties: winter melons.

Of the net-skinned melons, cantaloupes and Persian melons are the most well known. Although cantaloupe technically refers to an Italian hard-ridged and warted fruit, in the United States the term cantaloupe is applied to one of the most popular melon varieties. Persian melons are considered giant-sized versions of cantaloupes.

Winter melons are muskmelons that have smooth or wrinkled rinds but lack the ridged sections of the netted melons. They have been so named because they are late-season ripeners and can be stored during the winter months. Melon varieties that are included in this group are casaba, crenshaw, Christmas, and honeydew melons.

Watermelons stand in a category by themselves. The varieties commonly available are large or small, oblong or round, and red- or yellow-fleshed. The citron melon is a hard-fleshed watermelon used primarily for preserves and pickles.

How to select and store

Melon selection tends to perplex many homemakers, and rightly so. Although all exterior signs may indicate a sweet, juicy interior, the only sure way to tell if a melon is sweet or not is to sample its flesh. This is due to the close relationship between melon sweetness and weather conditions during maturation of the fruit on the vine. To add to the complexity of the problem, a mature melon is not necessarily a ripe one. Rather, maturity indicates that the melon will ripen properly under proper conditions.

Despite all of this confusion concerning melon selection, three very reliable indicators—the appearance of the stem end, the color of the rind, and the aroma of the melon—can guide the homemaker to select melons of the highest quality.

1. Cantaloupes and Persian melons should be ripened on the vine to what is called the "full slip" stage (the fruit separates cleanly from the vine). This leaves a clean, slightly indented scar at the stem end. Other melons, on the other hand, will have part of the stem attached to the fruit since they must be cut from the vines.

2. Because rind color changes as the melon ripens, know the ripe stage for each variety (see chart, page 1395).

3. A melon with pleasant, full-bodied aroma also indicates mature fruit. Only the casaba lacks an aroma.

Although softening at the blossom end is thought to be a way to tell maturity, this sign cannot be relied on. Repeated handling and application of pressure at this point will cause softening, also.

If the melon is to be used within a day or two, be sure to select a fully ripe one. If the melon is not fully ripe, let the mature fruit stand at cool room temperature for a few days in order for it to mellow. When the room begins to fill with a fragrant aroma from the melon, the time to refrigerate it has arrived.

When the melon is ripe, rinse and dry it off. Enclose the melon in a plastic bag or foil and refrigerate. Do not store near lettuce, carrots, celery, broccoli, butter, or other dairy products since these foods can absorb melon aroma. Use refrigerated ripe melons within three to five days.

		Know Your Melons		
Kind	Peak Seasons	Identifying Characteristics	Aroma and Flavor
Cantaloupe	June–August	Well-raised, coarsely netted rind with light green to yellow background. Slightly sunken, smooth scar at stem end. Salmon-colored flesh.	Pungent aroma; sweet.
Casaba	July–October	Globe-shaped; pointed stem end with part of stem attached. Butter yellow, wrinkled and furrowed rind. Soft, creamy white meat.	No aroma; mild, slightly sweet.
Christmas (Santa Claus)	December	Large, oblong shape. Green and gold rind. Yellow green flesh.	Mild, slightly sweet.
Crenshaw	July–October	Globe shape; pointed, slightly wrinkled stem attached. Shallow furrows. Rind green when immature; mottled yellow to yellow gold when ripe. Pink flesh.	Spicy, full aroma; juicy.
Honeydew and Honeyball	June–October	Oval to round. Slightly waxy, creamy yellow rind. Delicate green flesh. Honeyball smaller.	Pleasant aroma; sweet, juicy.
Persian	July–October	Resembles cantaloupe but larger size and more webbed than netted rind; smooth stem end; grayish green to brown background. Flesh orange to salmon pink.	Distinct aroma; mildly sweet.
Watermelon	May-August	Round to oval symmetrical shape. Solid deep green to gray rind with or without stripes; firm. Underside area yellow-tinged. Pinkish red or yellow flesh.	Juicy, sweet.

How to use

The sight and aroma of melons in the market is sure to arouse your taste buds. Wedged, sectioned, or sliced melons served alone or combined with other fruit can be served as the refreshing first, middle, or last course of breakfast, lunch, or dinner. (See also *Fruit*.)

Apple–Melon Toss

Combine 2½ cups cubed unpeeled apples, 1½ cups small cantaloupe *or* honeydew balls, and ½ cup sliced celery. Blend ½ cup dairy sour cream and ⅓ cup mayonnaise or salad dressing; stir in 2 ounces blue cheese, crumbled.

Add sour cream-mayonnaise dressing to fruit mixture; toss together lightly. Chill salad thoroughly. To serve, spoon the fruit salad into lettuce cups. Makes 4 or 5 servings.

Melon Wedges

Slice honeydew melons into quarters; scoop out seeds. Fill hollow with fresh blueberries and sliced bananas. Spoon Honey Dressing over.

Honey Dressing: Combine ½ cup dairy sour cream, ¼ teaspoon dry mustard, and 1½ to 2 tablespoons honey. Beat until ingredients are well blended. Add ½ teaspoon grated orange peel and dash salt; slowly beat in 1 tablespoon orange juice and 1 teaspoon lemon juice; chill mixture thoroughly. Makes ¾ cup.

Melon Salad

  1 3-ounce package cream cheese,
      softened
  2 tablespoons mayonnaise
  2 tablespoons milk
  ¼ cup diced celery
  2 tablespoons chopped pecans
  ½ cup frozen whipped dessert
      topping, thawed
  3 cups chilled melon balls

With rotary beater beat together first 3 ingredients till smooth and fluffy. Add celery and nuts; fold in thawed topping. Chill. Divide melon balls into 6 lettuce cups; top each serving with cheese mixture. Makes 6 servings.

Honeydew-Berry Parfaits

Quarter 2½ cups fresh strawberries, reserving 6 whole berries. Sprinkle cut berries with 1 tablespoon sugar. Mash 1 ripe, large banana. Blend in ½ cup plain yogurt, 2 teaspoons sugar, and ⅛ teaspoon ground cinnamon.

Arrange 2 cups diced fresh honeydew melon in bottoms of 6 parfait glasses; spoon *half* the yogurt mixture over. Top with sweetened berries; spoon remaining yogurt over berries. Garnish with reserved berries. Makes 6 servings.

Berried Melon Rings

  1 honeydew melon, chilled
  5 ounces prosciutto *or* corned beef,
      very thinly sliced
              . . .
  ½ cup dairy sour cream
  2 tablespoons confectioners'
      sugar
  2 cups blueberries

Remove rind from melon; cut a thin slice from bottom and top and discard. Cut melon into 6 crosswise slices; remove seeds. Cut the 2 smallest slices into cubes. Cut prosciutto into 1-inch wide strips; wrap 1 strip around each melon cube. Place a melon ring on each serving plate; top with melon cubes.

Stir together sour cream and confectioners' sugar; add berries. Spoon atop melon; trim with lettuce, if desired. Makes 4 servings.

Melon Supreme

  1 13½-ounce can pineapple tidbits
  1 cup small cantaloupe balls
  1 cup small watermelon balls
  1 cup sliced, peeled peaches*
  ¼ cup mayonnaise
  1 tablespoon confectioners' sugar
  ¼ teaspoon grated lemon peel
  ½ cup whipping cream

Drain pineapple, reserving 2 tablespoons syrup. Mix fruits; chill. Blend together reserved syrup, mayonnaise, and sugar; beat with rotary beater till smooth. Stir in lemon peel. Fold fruit into mayonnaise mixture. Whip cream; fold into fruit. Chill. Serves 6 to 8.

*To keep freshly cut fruit bright, use ascorbic acid color keeper or dip the cut fruit in lemon juice mixed with a little water.

Double-Decker Honeydew Mold

  2 envelopes unflavored gelatin
      (2 tablespoons)
  1 6-ounce can frozen lemonade
      concentrate, thawed
  2 7-ounce bottles ginger ale
      (about 2 cups)
  2 tablespoons maraschino
      cherry juice
  2 cups frozen honeydew balls,
      thawed and drained, or 2 cups
      fresh honeydew balls
  2 tablespoons sliced maraschino
      cherries
  ¼ cup dairy sour cream
  ¼ cup mayonnaise or salad dressing

Soften gelatin in ½ cup cold water. Add ¾ cup boiling water; stir till gelatin is dissolved. Stir in lemonade concentrate. Slowly add ginger ale, gently stirring with an up-and-down motion. Divide gelatin mixture in *half;* stir cherry juice into first half. Chill this half till partially set; fold in melon balls and cherries. Turn into 6½-cup mold; refrigerate.

Meanwhile, add sour cream and mayonnaise to second half of gelatin mixture. Beat with rotary beater till smooth; leave at room temperature till fruit layer in mold is *almost* firm. Pour sour cream mixture slowly over fruit layer. Chill till firm. Makes 8 to 10 servings.

Cantaloupe Crown

1 small cantaloupe, halved,
    seeded, and rind removed
1 3-ounce package lemon-lime
    flavored gelatin
1 3-ounce package lime-flavored
    gelatin
2½ cups boiling water
¼ cup lemon juice
    Dash salt

. . .

1 7-ounce bottle lemon-lime
    carbonated beverage, chilled
    (about 1 cup)

Cut cantaloupe in ¾-inch thick wedges. Dissolve gelatins in boiling water; stir in lemon juice and salt. Cool.

Pour carbonated beverage slowly into dissolved gelatin; stir gently to mix. Chill gelatin mixture till partially set. Arrange cantaloupe wedges in 6½-cup fluted tube mold. Carefully pour a *fourth* of the gelatin into mold. Chill gelatin in mold till *almost* firm. Leave remaining gelatin at room temperature.

Slowly pour *half* of remaining gelatin mixture into mold; chill till *almost* firm. Pour in remaining gelatin; chill till firm. Before unmolding, trim tips of cantaloupe if extending above gelatin. Makes 8 servings.

Saw-tooth cut melons serve as decorative bowls for salad mixtures. Crab Luncheon Salad is piled high in a Persian melon, while Buffet Fruit Medley warrants a watermelon shell.

Melon Polka-Dot Mold

    2 3-ounce packages cherry-
        flavored gelatin
    1 tablespoon lemon juice
    1 8-ounce package cream cheese
    ½ cup finely chopped pecans
    2 cups small melon balls

Dissolve gelatin in 2 cups boiling water. Stir in 1¾ cups cold water and lemon juice. Pour *1 cup* gelatin into 6½-cup ring mold. Chill till partially set. Shape cheese into 40 balls; roll in nuts. Arrange 9 cheese and 9 melon balls alternately in mold. Chill gelatin till *almost* firm. Meanwhile, chill remaining gelatin till partially set; fold in remaining cheese and melon balls. Pour over gelatin in mold. Chill till the mixture is firm. Makes 8 to 10 servings.

Coronado Salad

    2 medium cantaloupes, chilled
    2 cups diced cooked chicken
    ½ cup chopped celery
    ½ cup halved seedless green grapes
    2 tablespoons sliced pimiento-
        stuffed green olives
    ½ cup whipping cream
    ¼ cup mayonnaise or salad dressing
    4 clusters seedless green grapes
        Hard-cooked egg slices
        Toasted sliced almonds

Cut cantaloupes in half crosswise; remove seeds. Combine next 4 ingredients and ½ teaspoon salt, reserving a few olive slices; toss. Whip cream; fold in mayonnaise. Fold into chicken mixture. Spoon the mixture into melons. Garnish with remaining ingredients. Makes approximately 4 servings.

Luncheon Cooler

    2 medium cantaloupes, chilled
    2 medium peaches, peeled
    2 bananas, peeled and sliced*
    ½ cup fresh blueberries
    3 tablespoons honey
    2 to 3 teaspoons finely snipped
        candied ginger
        Lime sherbet

Cut cantaloupes in half crosswise; remove seeds. Slice *one* peach* and reserve for garnish. Dice remaining *peach** into large bowl. Add next 4 ingredients and toss lightly; spoon into cantaloupe halves. Arrange reserved peaches around each cantaloupe rim; top with a scoop of lime sherbet. Garnish with extra blueberries, if desired. Makes 4 servings.

*To keep cut fruit attractive and bright, use ascorbic acid color keeper or dip in lemon juice mixed with a little water.

Crab Luncheon Salad

    1 7½-ounce can crab meat, well
        drained and flaked
    ½ cup sliced celery
    2 tablespoons sliced pitted
        ripe olives
    1 tablespoon sliced green onion
    ½ cup mayonnaise or salad dressing
    3 hard-cooked eggs, sliced
    1 medium Persian melon, chilled

Combine first 4 ingredients, ¼ teaspoon salt, and dash pepper; fold in mayonnaise and *2* of the sliced eggs. Chill. Using a saw-tooth cut, remove top third of melon; remove seeds. Loosen melon meat from rind. Slice meat into sections and serve with salad. Sprinkle inside of melon with lemon juice. Fill melon hollow with salad. Trim with egg. Makes 4 servings.

Fruited Parfait Salad

Partially thaw and drain one 16-ounce package frozen sliced strawberries, one 10-ounce package frozen melon balls,* and one 10-ounce package frozen blueberries,* reserving ¼ cup strawberry syrup. Prepare dressing by blending together 1 cup dairy sour cream, reserved syrup, and ½ teaspoon grated lemon peel.

Allowing ⅓ cup cottage cheese for each salad, begin layering with *half* of one 16-ounce carton large curd cream-style cottage cheese in bottoms of 6 large parfait glasses. Continue layering with dressing, strawberries, a few melon balls, blueberries, remaining half carton of cottage cheese, dressing, and strawberries. Top parfaits with remaining melon balls. Serve immediately. Makes 6 servings.

*Substitute 1 cup fresh fruit, if desired.

Mint-laden Melon Tower combines the aromatic watermelon, cantaloupe, and honeydew flavors with the zest of citrus slices.

Melon Balls Melba

1 tablespoon cornstarch
¼ cup currant jelly
¼ cup rosé
6 drops almond flavoring
1 cup fresh raspberries,
    lightly sugared
3 cups cantaloupe balls

Blend 1 tablespoon water and cornstarch. Stir in jelly. Cook till jelly melts and mixture boils; remove from heat. Add next 3 ingredients. Cool. Spoon melon balls into sherbet glasses. Spoon on sauce. Garnish each serving with mint sprig, if desired. Makes 6 servings.

Raspberry-Melon Boats

Drain one 10-ounce package frozen red raspberries, thawed, reserving ½ cup syrup. To syrup add ½ cup orange juice. Mix 1 tablespoon cornstarch and 1 tablespoon sugar; gradually stir in syrup. Cook and stir till thickened and bubbly. Cool sauce; add berries.

Halve 1 small cantaloupe, chilled. Remove seeds and rind. Fill centers with scoops of vanilla ice cream. Drizzle sauce over. Serves 2.

Melon Tower

1 8-ounce package Neufchâtel
    cheese, softened
½ cup halved seedless green
    grapes
¼ cup broken pecans, toasted
1 slice chilled watermelon,
    about 6 inches in diameter
    and 2 inches thick
1 slice chilled honeydew melon,
    about 5 inches in diameter
    and 1½ inches thick
1 slice chilled cantaloupe
    about 4¾ inches in diameter
    and 1 inch thick
1 unpeeled orange, thinly sliced
1 unpeeled lemon, thinly sliced
1 unpeeled lime, thinly sliced
6 watermelon balls
6 tablespoons honey
¼ teaspoon grated lime peel
3 tablespoons lime juice
    Fresh mint sprigs

Beat cheese until light and fluffy. Fold in grapes and nuts; chill. Place watermelon on chilled plate. Top with honeydew, then cantaloupe.

Spoon cheese mixture into center of melon rings. Tuck oranges under edge of honeydew, lemons under cantaloupe. Halve lime slices and overlap in circle on top of cantaloupe. Insert 4 long, thin bamboo skewers through all tiers to hold tower in place. Pile watermelon balls in center of lime circle. (Assemble and fill tower just before serving or make about ½ hour ahead and refrigerate.)

Combine honey, lime peel, juice, and dash salt; serve with tower. Garnish the platter with mint sprigs. To serve, cut tower in quarters with serrated knife. Makes 4 servings.

Perfectly round melon balls are easy to make with a long-handled melon baller. Use scooped-out melon as a serving dish.

MELON BALL—A round piece of fruit scooped from the flesh of a melon. A special spoonlike utensil with a small rounded bowl is used to make melon balls.

Melon balls are an attractive and delicious addition to fresh fruit salads, compotes, gelatin salads, and punches.

MELT—To change a solid to a liquid by heating it. Butter and chocolate are frequently melted to make them easier to combine with other ingredients.

MENU—A complete list of the dishes to be served at a meal. At home, a menu is important both as a shopping and a cooking aid. Usually, this type of menu is not elaborate and is seen only by the homemaker. On the other hand, a restaurant menu or bill of fare is a complete list of all the dishes of the house along with the price of each. Exclusive restaurants often make their menus an elaborate showpiece.

Planning a nutritious and delicious menu requires artful juggling of family preferences, nutritional needs, time, and money. At first, this may entail concentrated effort, but it will become easier as you learn the techniques. (See *Meal Planning, Nutrition* for additional information.)

MERINGUE (*muh rang'*)—A mixture of egg whites and sugar that is beaten to a stiff foam, then either baked or poached. Cream of tartar is usually added to the unbeaten mixture to make the meringue more stable.

There are two basic types of meringue. A soft meringue, such as one that tops a cream pie, is baked quickly and has little sugar per egg white. A hard meringue is baked till crisp and has more sugar.

To many people, a cream pie seems incomplete unless it is topped with a soft meringue. Cookies, cakes, and other desserts also seem special when complemented with a soft meringue. This type of meringue may also be poached in milk and then served as a topping with a stirred custard or fruit cup dessert.

Soft meringues should be light and airy with no signs of shrinking. The following tips will help you achieve this kind of attractive and delicious meringue.

First of all, carefully separate the eggs so that no yolk gets mixed in with the egg white. Even a trace of fat from the yolk will prevent the whites from forming a stable foam. Also be sure that the beaters and mixing bowl are free of fat. (Remember: plastic mixing bowls may retain fat even after machine dishwashing.)

Beating the egg whites is the second step in making a meringue. There are two important things to remember: add the sugar gradually, and beat the foam long enough. The meringue is sufficiently beaten when the sugar is dissolved (no sugar crystals should be felt when you rub a little meringue between your fingers) and the peaks stand up when the beaters are lifted.

Now that the meringue is made, the last steps are spreading and baking it. If the

Refreshing summertime dessert

Delight guests by serving this crispy Me-→ ringue Shell piled high with Strawberry Sherbet made with fresh strawberries.

meringue is to top a cream pie, spread it on the hot filling as this helps reduce leakage and minimizes slipping. Prevent shrinkage of a soft meringue by sealing it to the edge of the pastry shell or baking dish. Then, bake the meringue-topped dessert in a moderate oven till the peaks of the meringue are golden brown.

Hard meringues are usually baked in a shallow cup shape and filled with a cream filling, fresh or canned fruit, ice cream, or a mixture of whipping cream and fruit which is piled high in the center.

The above rules about egg whites also apply to hard meringue. The real secret to success is baking this type of meringue slowly, then letting it dry in the still warm oven till crisp. (See also *Egg*.)

Meringue Shell

Use this as the base for a special dessert—

> 3 egg whites
> 1 teaspoon vanilla
> ¼ teaspoon cream of tartar
> Dash salt
> 1 cup sugar
> Ice cream and sauce *or* fresh fruit

Have egg whites at room temperature. Add vanilla, cream of tartar, and salt. Beat to soft peaks. Gradually add sugar, beating till very stiff peaks form and sugar is dissolved. (Meringue will still be glossy.)

Cover baking sheet with plain, *ungreased* brown paper. Using 9-inch round cake pan as guide, draw circle on paper. Spread meringue evenly over circle. Shape into shell with back of spoon, making bottom ½ inch thick and sides about 1¾ inches high. Bake at 275° for 1 hour. Turn off heat and let meringue shell dry in oven (door closed) for at least 2 hours. Fill with favorite ice cream and sauce *or* fresh fruit. Makes 8 servings.

Individual Meringue Shells: Make meringue as directed above. Cover baking sheet with plain, *ungreased* brown paper. Draw 8 circles, 3½ inches in diameter; spread each circle with ⅓ cup meringue. Using back of spoon, shape into shells. Bake at 275° for 1 hour. For crisper meringues, turn off heat and let dry in oven (door closed) 1 hour. Makes 8 servings.

Soft Meringue

For one 9-inch pie:

> 3 egg whites
> ½ teaspoon vanilla
> ¼ teaspoon cream of tartar
> 6 tablespoons sugar

For one 8-inch pie:

> 2 egg whites
> ½ teaspoon vanilla
> ¼ teaspoon cream of tartar
> 4 tablespoons sugar

Have egg whites at room temperature. Beat egg whites with vanilla and cream of tartar till soft peaks form. Gradually add sugar, beating till stiff and glossy peaks form and all of the sugar is dissolved. Spread meringue over the hot filling, sealing to the edge of the pastry. Bake at 350° till the meringue is golden, about 12 to 15 minutes. Cool thoroughly.

Note: Before cutting a meringue-topped pie, dip knife in water—no need to dry.

Strawberry Sherbet

> 1 *teaspoon* unflavored gelatin
> ¾ cup sugar
> Dash salt
> ½ cup water
> ½ cup pineapple juice
> 1 tablespoon lemon juice
> 1 quart fresh strawberries, crushed
> . . .
> Meringue Shell
> Marshmallow creme
> Fresh strawberry halves

In saucepan combine unflavored gelatin, sugar, and salt. Stir in water and pineapple juice. Stir over low heat till gelatin dissolves. Remove from heat; stir in lemon juice. Chill till partially set. Stir in crushed berries; pour into 1½-quart refrigerator tray. Partially freeze. Break into chunks; place in chilled bowl. Beat smooth with electric mixer. Return to tray; freeze till firm. Makes 1 quart.

Fill cooled Meringue Shell with sherbet. Top with marshmallow creme and berry halves.

Chewy Brownie Meringues are quick to make. Simply fold melted semisweet chocolate and nuts into the fluffy meringue base.

Pineapple Cream Pie

¾ cup sugar
¼ cup all-purpose flour
½ teaspoon salt
1 20½-ounce can crushed pineapple, undrained
1 cup dairy sour cream
1 tablespoon lemon juice
2 slightly beaten egg yolks
. . .
1 9-inch *baked* pastry shell, cooled (See *Pastry*)
Soft Meringue for 8-inch pie

In saucepan combine sugar, flour, and salt. Stir in pineapple, sour cream, and lemon juice. Cook and stir till mixture thickens and bubbles; cook and stir 2 minutes. Stir small amount hot mixture into yolks; return to hot mixture, stirring constantly. Cook and stir 2 minutes. Spoon into cooled pastry shell. Spread meringue atop pie, sealing to edge. Bake at 350° for 12 to 15 minutes. Cool before cutting.

Coffee Clouds

Beat 3 egg whites with 1 teaspoon vanilla, 1 teaspoon instant coffee powder, ¼ teaspoon cream of tartar, and dash salt to soft peaks. Gradually add 1 cup sugar, beating till stiff peaks form and the sugar is dissolved.

Cover baking sheet with plain *ungreased* brown paper. Draw eight 3½-inch circles; spread each circle with ⅓ cup meringue. Shape with back of spoon to make shells. Bake at 275° for 1 hour. For crisper meringue shells, turn off heat; let dry in oven (door closed) about 1 hour. Cool thoroughly before serving.

For filling combine one 6-ounce package butterscotch pieces (1 cup), 3 tablespoons water, 1 tablespoon instant coffee powder, and dash salt. Cook and stir over low heat till butterscotch pieces melt, then cook 1 to 2 minutes longer. Stir small amount hot mixture into 1 beaten egg; return to hot mixture. Cook and stir about 1 minute. Chill thoroughly.

Whip 1 cup whipping cream; fold in butterscotch mixture. Pile into meringue shells. Chill several hours. Trim with shaved unsweetened chocolate. Makes 8 servings.

Brownie Alaska

Cream together ¼ cup butter or margarine and 1 cup sugar till light and fluffy. Add 2 egg yolks, ¼ cup milk, and ½ teaspoon vanilla; beat well. Stir in two 1-ounce squares unsweetened chocolate, melted and cooled. Sift together ⅔ cup sifted all-purpose flour, ½ teaspoon baking powder, and ½ teaspoon salt; add to creamed mixture and mix well. Fold in 2 stiffly beaten egg whites.

Turn into greased and waxed paper-lined 9x 9x2-inch baking pan. Sprinkle with ⅓ cup chopped pecans. Bake at 350° for about 25 to 30 minutes. Remove from pan and cool. Trim to a 9x5-inch rectangle.

Beat 5 egg whites till soft peaks form. Gradually add ⅔ cup sugar, beating till stiff peaks form. Place brownie rectangle on a *wooden board;* top with 2 pints coffee ice cream, leaving a little of the brownie layer uncovered on all sides. Spread evenly with meringue, sealing carefully to brownie layer. Sprinkle top with ¼ cup finely chopped pecans. Bake at 450° till lightly browned, about 5 minutes. Serve immediately. Serves 8 to 10.

A smooth pineapple-sour cream filling complemented by the light, airy meringue make up this luscious Pineapple Cream Pie. Decorate the top by swirling the meringue before baking.

Brownie Meringues

A meringue cookie—

>   2 egg whites
>   Dash salt
> 1/2 teaspoon vinegar
> 1/2 teaspoon vanilla
> 1/2 cup sugar
>   1 6-ounce package semisweet
>   chocolate pieces (1 cup), melted
>   and cooled
> 3/4 cup chopped walnuts

Beat egg whites with salt, vinegar, and vanilla till soft peaks form. Gradually add sugar, beating to stiff peaks. Fold in melted chocolate and chopped walnuts. Drop from teaspoon onto greased cookie sheet. Bake at 350° about 10 minutes. Makes about 3 dozen cookies.

Prevent the meringue from shrinking by sealing it tightly to the pastry edge. A narrow spatula is handy for spreading.

Gently form Meringue Shells into a shallow cup shape with the back of a spoon. Use circles as guides for even-sized shells.

For an easy dessert, make Individual Meringue Shells ahead and top with a generous scoop of ice cream at serving time.

MEUNIÈRE BUTTER *(muhn yâr')*—A mixture of melted butter, lemon juice, and parsley that is usually served with fish.

MEXICAN COOKERY—Foods and food preparation techniques typical of Mexico. The cuisine of this south-of-the-border country is a conglomerate of dishes and cooking methods handed down by many generations of Mexicans blended with dishes introduced by the Spanish and others. This cuisine is characterized by spicy foods.

Historical influences: Centuries before Columbus sailed to the New World, the Mayans occupied what is now Mexico. Where these people came from is unknown, but it is apparent that they enjoyed a highly developed culture. They built towns with their stone tools and cultivated the food indigenous to the area. During the 1300s, the Aztecs, a tribe from the north, moved into southern Mexico. These highly civilized people, who dominated this area for 200 years, also found uses for many native foods, especially the cacao and vanilla beans.

Early in the sixteenth century, the Spanish, under Cortez, conquered Mexico. Among other things, they introduced rice, domestic pigs, goats, and wheat.

This Spanish influence was so strong that today many people think Spanish and Mexican cookery are identical. Although Spanish influence is present, many characteristics distinguish Mexican cooking, particularly the frequent use of hot chilies.

Still another food influence was exerted during the short reign of Emperor Maximilian (1864-1867), an Austrian who brought French support troops with him to Mexico. This resulted in the mingling of both French and Austrian cookery with the predominant Spanish-Mexican cuisine.

Despite these varied influences over such a long period of time, there has evolved a distinctive Mexican cuisine. It makes full use of foods native to Central and South America—particularly tomatoes, corn, *capsicum* peppers, beans, sweet potatoes and yams, avocados, and squashes—as well as the foods introduced by outsiders but now raised extensively in Mexico.

Well-known foods and recipes: Mexico is made up of highly diverse and often isolated geographic and cultural elements, so it is sometimes described as a large country made up of several small ones. In each area there is variation in food varieties and techniques. Nevertheless, the following Mexican foods and recipes have become accepted as being typically Mexican.

Since ancient times the multipurpose tortilla has been the bread of Mexico. Traditionally, corn kernels were boiled with lime to produce a soft mass called *mixtamal*. This was then ground into flour between two stones. From this dough flour, dough was made by adding water and salt. Today, however, tortilla dough flour, made of either corn or wheat, can be bought packaged. This product greatly shortens the time needed to make tortillas.

Tortillas are made into large or small, flat pancakes according to use. The large ones are cooked by frying to use as bread at a meal. Small tortillas are the basis for a number of truly Mexican foods.

For example, tacos are made by folding small tortillas, which have been fried in lard, over a filling of meat, cheese, sausage, or beans. If these small, flat, fried tortillas are topped with a meat or poultry mixture and a peppery sauce they become tostadas. And if you flavor the dough with cheese, chilies, or marrow and then make this into a turnover filled with ground meat, a chopped vegetable mixture, or peppers, mushrooms, or squash blossoms mixed with sausage, it becomes quesadillas.

Enchiladas are fried tortillas rolled around a pungently hot sausage and cheese mixture, lined up in a baking dish, covered with a chili pepper sauce, and topped with cheese and onion, then baked. When the tortillas are filled with a mixture of green chilies, green tomatoes, and fresh coriander and covered with a green chili sauce, they are called *enchiladas verdes,* the Mexican name for green enchiladas.

Like tortillas, tamales are made of dough flour. However, tamales have fat, leavening, and broth added to the dough. The dough is quite soft so that it can be spread on softened corn husk wrappings before cooking. Plain tamales are eaten as bread. For filled tamales, some sort of meat and chili sauce mixture is spread on the dough. Both types are rolled up in corn husks and steamed until the dough pulls away from the husk wrapper. Tamale dough is used, too, as a crust or topping for meat dishes.

Inseparable from most other cooking ingredients in Mexican cookery are the *capsicum* peppers called *chilies.* There are more than five dozen varieties of chilies available to Mexican cooks, but they use only about one dozen to any large extent. After discarding the seeds, which may be hot even if the flesh is not, green or red sweet chilies are used fresh.

However, both red and green chilies are also used dried. Dried, red *capsicums* vary from mild and flavorful to very hot and pungent, while green chilies are often hotter than are the red ones. Like fresh peppers, the heat of dried peppers can be somewhat tamed by removing the seeds before using. If the chilies are pickled, reduce the hotness by washing them.

Mexican cooks choose specific chilies by name to give the fiery or mild flavor that they desire in a dish. Powdered chilies are also used, but they must not be confused with chili powder mixtures which are an entirely different type of seasoning made of a blend of spices.

Chilies and sauces should be mentioned together, since few Mexican sauces are made without some chili. One typically Mexican chili sauce is molé, which is made in various ways. Red molé contains ripe tomatoes and red chilies, while green molé has green tomatoes, green chilies, and fresh coriander leaves. The most exotic Mexican molé sauce is *molé poblano,* a red chili sauce containing bitter chocolate. This sauce is used for turkey, tacos, or a chicken and tortilla casserole. The chocolate flavor loses itself in the mixture but subtly adds to the distinctive overall flavor.

Unlike molé sauces which are cooked with foods, two sauces—*salsa cruda* and *salsa verde*—are almost always on the table at meals, to be added at will to meat dishes or soups. *Salsa cruda* is a red sauce made of uncooked tomatoes, green chilies, and herbs, while *salsa verde* is a mixture of green tomatoes, green chilies, and garlic.

Well known outside Mexico as a dip is guacamole, an avocado-based mixture that serves as a sauce and a salad in Mexico.

Beans, known as frijoles, are a staple Mexican food. Red kidney, pink, speckled, yellow, pinto, and black beans, chosen according to taste, are cooked with chilies and other seasonings, then mashed to serve as a side dish. When the mashed beans are cooked with lard to a smooth paste, they are *frijoles refritos* or refried beans.

The meats most frequently used in Mexican dishes are pork and beef. Pork is typically cooked in a green or red, puréed chili sauce to make *adobo,* or in a thick sauce of chopped ingredients to make a kind of stew called *tinga*. Mexican cooks also prepare pork pieces with pineapple, mint, and just a touch of chili; with sausages and almonds; with tart apples, mustard, and wine, as well as in a dozen other ways. Beef is often cooked with beans and chilies to make chili con carne. It is also stewed with garlic and chilies, sauced several ways, and braised and jelled with orange juice, herbs, and spices. Steak is smothered with sweet carrots and made into *picadillo*.

Although beef and pork are Mexican favorites, other meats, poultry, fish, and eggs are also used to add variety. For example, a whole lamb is occasionally barbecued in a pit lined with century plant or banana leaves. Roast kid is sometimes the meat for a festive meal. Both chicken and turkey are stewed, braised, sauced, smothered with vegetables, stuffed, or fried. Parts of Mexico, particularly along the coast, have an abundance of fish and shellfish. Fish are poached, fried, or baked in a sauce, always with chilies for seasoning as well as herbs and spices. Often, nuts are added for texture and flavor. Eggs are scrambled in sauce or with pieces of cactus, fried to top tortillas, or combined with seafood and vegetables in a main dish.

Desserts are quite important to Mexican cookery, perhaps because they soothe the tongue from the bite of fiery foods. From the Spanish came caramel flan, a baked, syrup-coated custard, which is now a Mexican favorite. *Almendrado* is a delicately molded almond and egg white pudding served with an almond sauce. For sweet fritters, there are *sopapillas* shaped like small puffy pillows and sprinkled with sugar and cinnamon. Some sweet and creamy Mexican rice puddings contain nuts; others are delicately flavored with wine. One of the spectacular Mexican desserts is the King's Day (Epiphany) Ring. This yeast cake is rich in egg yolks and butter and well filled with candied fruits and peels.

Notches

Arrange tortilla chips on baking sheet. Place 1 teaspoon canned bean dip, small square of Cheddar cheese, and chopped chili pepper on each. Broil till cheese melts, 1 to 3 minutes.

Tostada Casserole

Convenience ingredients make this Mexican-style casserole quick to prepare —

    1 pound ground beef
    1 15-ounce can tomato sauce
       (2 cups)
    1 envelope taco seasoning mix
  2½ cups corn chips
    1 15½-ounce can refried beans
    2 ounces natural Cheddar cheese,
       shredded (½ cup)

In skillet brown ground beef. Add *1½ cups* tomato sauce and taco seasoning mix, stirring to mix well. Line bottom of 11¾x7½x1¾-inch baking dish with *2 cups* corn chips; crush remaining corn chips and set aside.

Spoon meat mixture over corn chips in baking dish. Combine remaining tomato sauce and refried beans; spread over ground beef mixture. Bake at 375° till mixture is heated through, about 25 minutes. Sprinkle with shredded cheese and crushed corn chips; bake till cheese is melted, about 5 minutes more. Makes 6 servings.

Cottage Enchiladas

    1 4-ounce can green chilies
   12 canned or frozen tortillas
             . . .
    1 cup dairy sour cream
    1 12-ounce carton cream-style
       cottage cheese (1½ cups)
   ½ teaspoon salt
     Dash pepper
   ½ pound sharp process American
       cheese, cut in 12 strips
    1 15-ounce can enchilada sauce

Drain chilies; remove seeds, if desired. Cut chilies into 12 strips. Cook tortillas according to package directions. Combine sour cream, cottage cheese, salt, and pepper. Reserve ½ cup of the mixture; spoon remaining mixture onto tortillas. Top each with a strip of green chili and a strip of cheese; roll up. Place, seam-side down, in 12x7½x2-inch baking dish.

Combine reserved sour cream mixture and enchilada sauce; pour over tortillas. Bake at 350° for 25 to 30 minutes. Garnish with ripe olives, if desired. Makes 6 servings.

Mexican Enchiladas

12 canned or frozen tortillas
⅓ cup salad oil
. . .
1 10-ounce can enchilada sauce
Cheese Sauce
4 tomatoes, peeled and diced
(about 2 cups)
½ cup finely chopped onion

Fry tortillas in hot salad oil, one at a time, just till they are softened, about 5 seconds on each side; drain. Heat the enchilada sauce; dip tortillas in the sauce. Spoon 1 to 2 tablespoons Cheese Sauce on each tortilla; sprinkle with about 2 tablespoons tomato and 2 teaspoons onion; roll up. Place the enchiladas, seam side down, in a greased 12x7½x2-inch baking dish. Combine remaining Cheese Sauce and enchilada sauce; pour over casserole. Bake at 350° for about 25 minutes. Makes 6 servings.

Cheese Sauce: Melt ¼ cup butter or margarine; blend in ¼ cup flour, ½ teaspoon salt, and ¼ teaspoon paprika. Add 2 cups milk; cook, stirring constantly, till sauce thickens and bubbles. Blend in 6 ounces sharp process American cheese, shredded (1½ cups), and 3 drops bottled hot pepper sauce.

Christmas Eve Salad

2 apples, sliced
1 banana, sliced
Lemon juice
1 16-ounce can sliced beets,
drained
1 20½-ounce can pineapple chunks,
drained
2 oranges, sectioned
Lettuce
. . .
½ cup peanuts
Pomegranate seeds
Mayonnaise or salad dressing
Milk

Sprinkle apples and bananas with a little lemon juice to prevent darkening. Arrange beets and fruits on lettuce-lined platter. Sprinkle peanuts and pomegranate seeds over top. Pass mayonnaise or salad dressing thinned with a little milk. Makes 6 to 8 servings.

Easy-to-prepare Mexicali Casserole is made from convenience foods—canned tamales, hominy, Vienna sausages, and soup.

Mexicali Casserole

1 20-ounce can yellow hominy
1 16-ounce can tamales, cut in
thirds
1 4- or 5-ounce can Vienna sausages,
cut in thirds
1 10½-ounce can condensed cream
of chicken soup
1 ounce sharp natural Cheddar
cheese, shredded (¼ cup)

Drain hominy; combine with next 3 ingredients. Turn into 1½-quart casserole. Bake, uncovered, at 350° for 35 to 40 minutes. Sprinkle cheese atop. Return to oven to melt cheese. Serves 6.